Business Plan In A Day

D0725244

Business Plan In A Day

Get it done right, get it done fast™

**Rhonda Abrams
and Guy Clapperton**

with Julie Vallone

CAPSTONE

Business Plan In A Day
Contents

About the Authors

Rhonda Abrams is a syndicated columnist, best-selling author, and popular public speaker. She has spent more than fifteen years advising, mentoring, and consulting with entrepreneurs and small business owners. Her knowledge of the small business market and her passion for entrepreneurship have made her one of the USA's most recognised advocates for small business.

An experienced entrepreneur, Rhonda has started three successful companies, including a small business planning consulting firm. Her experience gives her a strong real-life understanding of the challenges facing entrepreneurs. Currently, she is the founder and CEO of The Planning Shop, a company focused on providing entrepreneurs with high-quality information and tools for developing successful businesses.

Guy Clapperton contributed regularly to the *Guardian*'s Business Sense section for small businesses throughout its eight-year run as columnist, editorial associate and podcaster. Before this he ran a newsletter focusing on small business issues and continues to be fascinated by entrepreneurialism.

Currently, Guy writes business articles for the *Guardian*, *Financial Times*, *Esquire* and numerous other publications. He also writes for *The Times*, *The Sunday Times*, *Independent*, *Mail on Sunday*, *Radio Times* and other national publications. He broadcasts occasionally for BBC Radio London and the BBC World Service, normally about technology.

The *In A Day* Promise
Get it done right, get it done fast

You're busy. We can help.

The Planning Shop is dedicated to helping entrepreneurs create and grow successful businesses. As entrepreneurs ourselves, we understand the many demands placed on you. We don't assume that you're a dummy, just that you're short on time.

This *In A Day* book will enable you to complete a critical business task in a hurry —and in the right way. You'll get it done right and get it done fast.

Can you complete this project in just twenty-four hours? Yes. Perhaps the twenty-four hours won't be consecutive. You may start—pause for an hour, day, or week to take care of other business—then return to the task later. Or, you may have some research or other preparation to do before you can complete this project.

We'll guide you through the process, show you what you absolutely have to do, and give you tips and tricks to help you reach your goals. We've talked to the experts and done the research so you don't have to. We've also eliminated any unnecessary steps so you don't waste your valuable time. That's the *In A Day* promise.

When you have a business task you need to do *now*, the *In A Day* books will help you get it done—in as little as a day.

Need a Business Plan Fast?
This Book Is For You!

You need a business plan—fast!

Maybe a potential investor has asked to see your plan by Tuesday. Perhaps you need a business plan to present at an upcoming staff meeting. Possibly you just want to get your business off the ground as quickly as possible.

Business Plan In A Day was created for busy people like you. This book delivers the critical, time-tested information and tools you need to develop a well-constructed and effective plan—quickly and efficiently.

Business Plan In A Day was designed to help you successfully achieve your goal. It's for people who need a business plan to:

● Seek financing from a bank or other lender

● Approach investors, such as angel investors or venture capitalists

● Create a new business

● Expand an existing business

● Report to management on department or team plans

● Set goals with, inform, and motivate team members or employees

● Enter a business plan competition or complete a college business plan project

● Plan the strategy and direction of a company

An effective business plan saves you time and money by focusing your business activities. It can give you control over your finances, marketing, and daily operations. A good plan can also help you raise the money you need to build your company. *Business Plan In A Day* gives you everything you need to get it done right—and get it done fast!

Not sure what business to start?

Find tips and suggestions in *What Business Should I Start?*, available at bookshops and online.

Want to learn more about business concepts and business plans?

For even more on business planning and business plans, see *The Successful Business Plan*, available at bookshops and online.

Overview:
What's a Business Plan?

Your business plan is a powerful document telling the story of your company. It presents your current position, your vision for the future, and your plans for realising that vision.

A business plan answers the following questions:

- What is your business idea or what is your existing business?

- Who are your existing and/or potential customers and what motivates them to buy from you?

- How will you let your customers know about your business?

- Who are your competitors and how are you different from them?

- How will you carry out the basic functions of your business?

- Is your management team capable of guiding your business to success?

- What is the long-term future of your business?

- What is your company's financial picture? How much money will it cost to run your business and how much money will you make?

Anatomy of a Business Plan

The basic parts of a complete business plan are:

- **Executive Summary**: Highlights the most important aspects of your business, summarising key points of your business plan.

- **Company Description:** Features the basic, factual details about your business.

- **Target Market Description:** Identifies the types of people or businesses most likely to be your customers, and explains their needs and wants.

- **Competitive Analysis**: Evaluates other companies offering a similar product or service or filling a similar market need.

- **Marketing and Sales Plan:** Outlines how you will reach your customers and secure orders or make sales.

- **Operations Plan**: Explains how you run your business and the operational factors that may give you an edge over your competition.

- **Management Team:** Describes the key people running your business.

- **Development Plan and Milestones:** Shows where your business will be in several years' time, how you will get there, and the milestones you plan to reach along the way.

- **Financials.** A set of financial statements showing the current financial status and future financial goals of your company.

Although the Executive Summary appears first in your plan, prepare it last. You'll find it much easier to put together when you can draw from the highlights of each previously completed section.

Business Plan In A Day guides you quickly and efficiently through the process of developing a business plan. It's a roadmap to your success.

Time-Saving Tools

You probably already have a number of documents that will enable you to complete your plan faster. These include:

- Industry information, statistics, and data
- Surveys and other research about your target customers
- Information about your competition, including research from their websites
- Marketing brochures and other marketing materials
- Any past internal company planning papers
- Past tax returns (for existing companies)
- Organisational charts
- Charts depicting operational procedures
- Product data sheets

At the beginning of each step in this book, you'll find checklists showing the kinds of documents and other materials likely to provide helpful information for each section.

Using the Book

Throughout this book you'll see samples from the business plan of the fictional company ComputerEase. Next to them you'll find worksheets where you can jot down and organise the information about your own company. By the time you finish each worksheet, you'll have all the information necessary for your own business plan.

The ComputerEase sample plan sections (based on a fictional company) illustrate how particular sections of a completed business plan might look. The sample plans are in an abbreviated form due to space limitations; your own plan may be longer.

MARKET TRENDS

The Scottish economy is expanding. According to the Office of National Statistics, in the last four years the number of salaried employees in the area has increased by over 50,000. A survey by *The Scotsman* showed that 43 per cent of companies intended to add employees in the next 24 months.

Promising trends

Use the worksheets to write down the information about your own company that you'll need to complete your plan. If there's not enough space on the worksheets, use a separate piece of paper to record your thoughts and data.

What is the rate of growth of your target market?

What changes are occurring in the makeup of the market? (Include changes in technology, the economy, social values and concerns.)

How to
Use This Book

Business *Plan In A Day* outlines the key elements of a business plan in a step-by-step guide, showing you what to include—and what to leave out—in every section of your plan. Within each step, you'll find the tools to help you complete your own personal plan, including:

- Checklists outlining what you will accomplish in each step

- 'Time-Saving Tools' showing what information, if you have it, will let you finish the task faster

- Worksheets that help you organise data about your own company for each section of your plan

- A sample business plan showing what the parts of your plan might look like

- QuickTips, Sidebars, and Keys to Success to help you make certain your plan is done right

At the end of the book, we show you how to put it all together. A presentation and layout section explains how you can design your plan to achieve the best results.

You'll also find interviews with four experts who read and judge business plans every day—two private equity investors, a venture capitalist and a business angel. These real-life professionals give valuable insights into what makes a winning plan, and they share the common mistakes that can lead to rejection.

Finally, a 'Resources' section helps you locate a funding source for your venture by offering a list of groups and associations that provide business financing, as well as a variety of resources for entrepreneurs.

From the step-by-step plan-building guidelines to the valuable 'Keys to Success', *Business Plan In A Day* is your one-stop resource for creating a successful business plan. Our goal: to help get your plan done, get it done right, and get it done fast.

1

STEP 1: **Executive Summary**

STEP 2: Company Description

STEP 3: Target Market

STEP 4: The Competition

STEP 5: Marketing and Sales Plan

STEP 6: Operations

STEP 7: Management Structure

STEP 8: Future Development

STEP 9: Financials

Accomplishments

In this step you'll:

☐ 1. Prepare your Executive Summary

Time-Saving Tools

You'll complete this section more quickly if you have any of the following handy:

☐ Information about your potential business plan readers
☐ Completed worksheets for Steps 2–9

Step 1:
Executive Summary

Your Executive Summary is the single most important part of your business plan—particularly if you are seeking outside funding. Busy investors and lenders start reading here and use the Executive Summary to get an understanding of your business quickly.

In fact, some investors ask entrepreneurs to first send only their Executive Summary and financial statements (Step 9). If they like what they see, they'll request the full plan. So if you can hook your readers here, they'll ask for more. Your goal is to both summarise the major components of your business and to make your readers want to learn more.

This doesn't mean you can misrepresent your business. As in all parts of your business plan, the information you present in your Executive Summary must be truthful. But you can, and should, focus on those aspects of your business that show it in the very best light.

Your Executive Summary provides a *brief* snapshot of your business. Highlight the most important facts and concepts from your full business plan as concisely as possible. When completed, your Executive Summary will answer these questions for your readers:

- Does your basic concept make sense?
- Has your business been thoroughly planned?
- Is the management team capable?
- Is there a clear-cut market need for your product/service?
- What advantages do you have over your competition?
- Are your financial projections realistic?
- Is the business likely to succeed?
- Will investors be able to make money? Will lenders be able to get their money back, and when?

⚙ KEY TO SUCCESS
First Things Last!

Even though your Executive Summary comes first in your business plan, you'll find it much easier to prepare—and much more compelling—if you write it last. Once you've completed the rest of your plan on the pages that follow, you'll find it much faster to come back and produce this section.

Visualise your reader

As you create your Executive Summary, ask yourself, 'Who's going to read my business plan?' You can improve your chances of getting a positive reaction if you keep your potential business plan reader in mind as you write.

Remember, your reader is only going to spend a few minutes on your Executive Summary. They're going to home in on the issues that concern them most. If you understand their priorities, you'll be better able to craft it to push just the right buttons.

What Sets You Apart?

Think about the number of business plans your readers must plough through each day, especially if they're investors or bank lenders. (An average venture capitalist, for instance, usually sees about 1,000 plans a year.) What distinguishes yours from the rest of the stack? Highlight the qualities that set you apart from all the other businesses early on in your Executive Summary. Put your winning concept up front and make sure your readers get it.

Do some homework to discover the interests and concerns of your likely business plan reader. Then put those issues near the top of your Executive Summary. A venture capitalist might want to see that you have ground-breaking new technology, and an angel investor might want to see that you've identified an easily reached target market, while a banker wants to know that the company owners are investing their own money in the business. Give more emphasis to those aspects that concern your reader most.

Of course, you might not be able to identify the particular person who's going to read your plan. In that case, you can focus on the *type* of person and their concerns. For instance, a banker is likely to look for aspects of your business plan that minimise risk, since they want to make sure their loan will be secure. An investor, on the other hand, looks for aspects that increase the chance that your company will grow large, since they will get a piece of the action. Refer to the interviews with investors and lenders in *The Experts Speak* on pages **155–165** to get a better idea of how each type of reader reviews business plans.

1. Prepare your summary

Your Executive Summary is the single most important part of your business plan. Readers will review it before they read any other section. Many readers will breeze through the Executive Summary, so you need to explain your business concept clearly, concisely, and in a way that makes them want to know more. Your Executive Summary is the first impression many readers will get of your company. Make sure it's a good one.

On pages 8–10, you'll find a worksheet to help you prepare your Executive Summary. Each question on the worksheet refers to corresponding worksheets throughout this book. You'll find it much easier—and quicker—to complete the Executive Summary worksheet if you've already worked through the rest of the steps in this book (Steps 2–9). Just refer to your completed worksheets to assemble the key ingredients for an informative, compelling Executive Summary.

Before you get to the worksheets you'll see a sample Executive Summary for the fictional company ComputerEase. Review this model for more ideas about the content and structure of an Executive Summary.

🛈 KEY TO SUCCESS

Pay Attention to Presentation!

A few ways to make your Executive Summary look appealing to readers:

- Divide the Summary into paragraphs that mirror the sections of your business plan.

- Keep each topic brief.

- Use bullets to highlight your most compelling information.

- Include a small chart or graph if it makes an important point clear.

- Use white space and informative subheads to break up text blocks and make the pages seem less intimidating.

For additional suggestions, see *Presentation Pointers* on page 141.

EXECUTIVE SUMMARY

Immediately highlights a positive factor

THE COMPANY

ComputerEase Limited, an Edinburgh-based company, provides computer software training services to corporations in Scotland. The technology-related business services industry in the UK is one of the fastest areas of growth, and ComputerEase intends to capitalise on that. The company's stock is currently held by president and CEO Scott Connors and marketing director, Susan Alexander.

Provides basic company details in a straightforward style

PRODUCTS AND SERVICES

The company provides software training programmes targeted at the corporate market. Classes are conducted either at the customer's place of business or at ComputerEase's Corporate Training Centre. Additionally, weekend classes are offered to the general public. Training is offered for all leading software programmes. ComputerEase will also devise custom programmes at corporate customers' request.

Briefly describes the company's offerings

TARGET MARKET

ComputerEase operates in the Edinburgh area, targeting large- and medium-sized businesses with high computer use. Edinburgh is the capital city of Scotland with a diverse and healthy economy. The Office of National Statistics show that more than 5000 companies and institutions with more than fifty employees (ComputerEase's primary target market) are located in the area.

Shows large market potential

THE COMPETITION

No market leaders have yet emerged in the corporate software training field in Edinburgh. Competition is diverse and uneven, creating substantial market opportunities. ComputerEase maintains the following advantages over existing competition: company-owned, up-to-date computer training centre; local sales staff with strong ties to target customers; certification and strategic partnerships with leading software publishers; ongoing post-training customer support.

Describes competitive edge

MARKETING AND SALES STRATEGY

ComputerEase differentiates itself in its marketing by emphasising the needs of the corporation, not merely the students in the training classes. The company employs a highly regarded sales professional with extensive ties to the target market. ComputerEase secures sales predominantly through face-to-face approaches, unlike national competitors who rely on mail or telesales.

OPERATIONS

ComputerEase owns its own Corporate Training Centre with twelve personal computer stations fully equipped with all the latest versions of the most-used business software programmes. The company offers corporate training sessions at the Centre, as well as at the customer's place of business. It plans to open a second Training Centre with funds currently being sought. ComputerEase utilises the excess capacity of the Training Centre by offering Saturday classes to consumers. All equipment is leased, resulting in lower capital expenses and ensuring the latest in equipment at all times.

MANAGEMENT

President and founder Scott Connors brings significant technology-related management experience to this position. Immediately before starting ComputerEase, Connors served as regional manager for Wait's Computer Emporium, a large computer hardware and electronics retail chain. Earlier, he was a sales representative for IBM. Director Susan Alexander brings relevant experience in marketing to, and contacts with, the target market from her prior position as assistant marketing director for AlwaysHere Health Care Plan and sales experience as sales representative for SpeakUp Dictation Equipment.

> Highlights management's relevant experience

DEVELOPMENT

In the future, the company may become a franchise operation, or expand its own company-owned and operated training centres throughout the UK. The company's goal is to become the dominant regional corporate software training provider.

FINANCIALS

The financial strategy of ComputerEase emphasises reinvestment of income for growth during the first few years of operation, with the company reaching profitability by year three. Annual turnover projections for the current year are £233,000; for year two, £493,875; and for year three, £818,615.

FUNDS SOUGHT AND USES

The company is currently seeking £80,000 in investment financing. These funds will be used for expansion activities, including opening an additional Training Centre, hiring new staff, and increasing marketing activities. Long-term plans call for the company to either develop a franchise operation or expand to become a regional chain, adding at least one training location annually. The company would then also be an excellent candidate for acquisition by a national training company.

> Provides specific numbers and uses of funds. Hints at exit opportunity

What is your business all about? What are its most compelling qualities? Answer the questions on this worksheet, summarising conclusions you've reached in the worksheets in steps 2–9 of this book. Organise the information in a way that most appeals to your target reader. Combine related topics if that improves the flow.

THE COMPANY

What are the basic details of your business? (See worksheets on pages 15 and 17.)

_____

_____

_____

_____

_____

_____

PRODUCTS AND SERVICES

What products/services do you offer or plan to offer? (See worksheet on page 21.)

_____

_____

_____

_____

_____

_____

TARGET MARKET

Who are your customers? (Include a summary of any market research results.)
(See worksheet on page 42.)

_____

_____

_____

_____

_____

_____

THE COMPETITION

Who are your competitors? How is the market currently divided? What gives your company its competitive edge? (See worksheet on page 58.)

MARKETING AND SALES STRATEGY

How will you market and sell your product? (See worksheet on page 70.)

OPERATIONS

What are your most important operational features? (See worksheet on page 82.)

MANAGEMENT

Who are your founders? Who are the key members of your management team and what are their qualifications? (See worksheet on page 96.)

DEVELOPMENT

What is the company's current stage of development? What are your long-term goals? What are some of the milestones you've met or plan to meet? What is your potential exit strategy? (See worksheet on page 110.)

_____

_____

_____

_____

_____

_____

FINANCIALS

What are the expected financial highlights/performance of your company? What are your company's expected gross sales and net profits? (Use gross sales and net profit figures from the worksheets on pages 122–123.)

_____

_____

_____

_____

_____

FUNDS SOUGHT AND USES

How much money are you seeking, from what sources, and how will the money be used? (See worksheets on pages 25 and 137.)

_____

_____

_____

_____

_____

_____

Accomplishments

In this step you'll:

- ☐ 1. List your company's name(s) and location(s)
- ☐ 2. Provide information about your company's ownership and legal structure
- ☐ 3. Describe your company's history, development stage, and milestones
- ☐ 4. Describe your product(s) and service(s)
- ☐ 5. Give an overview of your industry
- ☐ 6. Explain how your company has been funded to date and how much money you are seeking

Time-Saving Tools

You'll complete this section more quickly if you have any of the following handy:

- ☐ Business license(s), incorporation papers, or other key business documents
- ☐ Legal and financial agreements
- ☐ Product or service descriptions
- ☐ Dates of key developments in your company's history
- ☐ Industry research data

Step 2:
Company Description

The Company Description provides the basic details about your business. While your Executive Summary creates a compelling case for why your business will succeed, the Company Description fills in the necessary specifics.

While much of this information seems—and is—mundane, providing these facts is the foundation of the picture you paint of your company. Completing this section should not be particularly time consuming or cumbersome; the goal is to quickly provide background information about your company's structure, ownership, and developments to date.

This section also provides a glimpse of what's going on in your industry. Offering an overview of your industry is particularly important if it is going through significant changes or facing economic difficulties. You'll need to show you understand the challenges your business, as part of that industry, faces. Of course, if your industry is healthy and growing, you'll want to point out those positive trends.

1. Give your company name(s) and location(s)

In the introductory section of your company description, include the basic details you'd put on any business application or form.

To begin, provide all the names associated with your company. In many cases, the name of your company or corporation is not the same as the name(s) you use when doing business with the public. You may actually have a number of different 'names' associated with your business, including:

- Your own name

- If incorporated, the company name

- A T/A (trading as)—or 'trading name'— also known as a 'fictitious business name'

- Brand name(s)

- The name of your website

- Subsidiary companies

For instance, a restaurant called 'Carla's Trattoria' might be legally owned by a corporation named C & J Food Enterprises. 'Carla's Trattoria' is the trading name of the company, and both names should be listed in the business plan. If the restaurant's owners also bottle and sell spaghetti sauce, the name of the brand of their bottled foods ('Carla's Special Sauces') should also be listed.

List the location of your company's main place of business, any branch locations, and any other locations, such as warehouses. If you operate more than two or three branches, you can list the total number of locations here, but include a complete list of addresses in your business plan's appendix.

COMPANY NAME AND LOCATION

ComputerEase Ltd. is an Edinburgh-based company providing computer software training services to business customers in Scotland, operating under the name 'ComputerEase'.

Corporate headquarters and the company's software training classrooms are located at 43 Priory Street, Edinburgh. ComputerEase also offers software training classes at its corporate clients' offices.

Name(s) of business

Company address and location where they conduct business

What are the names associated with your company? (List all company names, including the legal name of the corporation, trading name, brand or product names, names of subsidiaries, and domain names.)

_____

_____

_____

_____

Where is the company's main place of business? (Give the specific address, if known, or the general area or city if a location is yet to be selected.)

_____

_____

_____

_____

Do you have more than one location? (If so, list the addresses of each. If the company has many locations, list the total number and addresses or areas where they're located.)

_____

_____

_____

_____

_____

2. Provide information about your company's ownership and legal status

Who owns your company? If yours is a one-person business, the answer may be simple: you do. But if you have gone into business with others, you need to spell out the ownership division and indicate the names of all major shareholders.

It's also important to specify the legal form of your business, especially if you're seeking financing. Your funders want to know what type of entity they're doing business with. Many businesses often start out as one form of business (such as sole proprietor) and decide to incorporate later.

Other legal considerations to note here include:

- Licensing and distribution agreements

- Trademarks, copyrights and patents

- Other legal protections you have secured to protect your proprietary business assets

- Other legal issues having a major impact on your business

What's Your Legal Status?

Sole Trader: The company is not incorporated and is owned and managed by one person.

Partnership: A relationship in which two or more people own a company, sharing profits, losses and, usually, management. You can legally be deemed to be in a partnership even if you have not drawn up legal partnership documents.

Limited Liability Partnership (LLP): Similar to a partnership except that the exposure to financial risk is limited to the money the partners have put into the organisation. So if things go badly nobody can chase you for personal money or assets. Members are taxed on their share of profits.

Limited Liability Company: A limited liability company is a legal entity in its own right, so its money is separate from that of the owner. The reporting obligations are more stringent than for non-incorporated companies. There are two main sorts: private limited companies and public limited companies (plc), the latter being listed on a Stock Exchange.

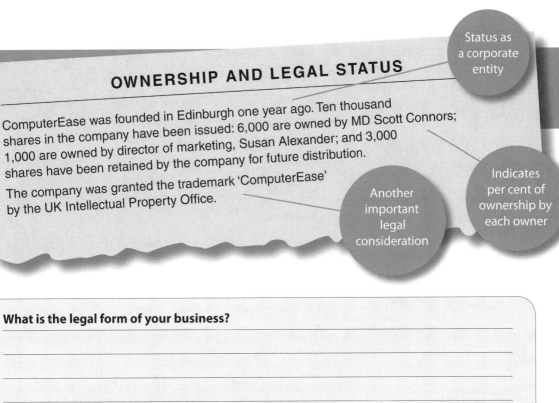

OWNERSHIP AND LEGAL STATUS

ComputerEase was founded in Edinburgh one year ago. Ten thousand shares in the company have been issued: 6,000 are owned by MD Scott Connors; 1,000 are owned by director of marketing, Susan Alexander; and 3,000 shares have been retained by the company for future distribution.

The company was granted the trademark 'ComputerEase' by the UK Intellectual Property Office.

Status as a corporate entity

Indicates per cent of ownership by each owner

Another important legal consideration

What is the legal form of your business?

Who owns your company? If the company has more than one owner, what percentage of the company does each own? If the company is incorporated, who owns the stock and in what amounts?

What trademarks, copyrights or patents does the company hold?

What other important legal issues affect the company? (Distribution or licensing agreements? Major lawsuits? Regulatory concerns?)

QUICK**TIP**

**Examples of
Key Milestones**

- Incorporation

- Prototype completed

- First product shipped

- Major customers secured

- Key strategic partnerships
  secured

- Significant sales level
  reached

3. Describe your company's history, development stage and milestones

Your company's history and milestones may make up the bulk of the Company Description portion of your business plan. In this section, you present the history and progress of your company.

First, indicate which phase of development your business is in. The basic stages are:

- **Seed company**. The business concept is developed, but the product or service is not yet finalised. Not yet making sales.

- **Start-up**. In the early stages of operation. Securing first customers.

- **Expanding**. Established company adding new products, services or branches. Rapidly increasing sales growth.

- **Stable**. Established company with modest ongoing sales growth.

- **Retrenchment**. Consolidating or repositioning product lines. Little or no sales growth.

Next, indicate the progress you've already made. Even if yours is a new business, you've almost certainly reached key milestones, such as developing a product prototype, securing seed financing, or finding office space. Be sure to include development details that indicate you're off to a good start.

If your company is up and running, you already have some major accomplishments under your belt, such as reaching significant sales levels, securing major customers, or shipping products. Highlight these in this portion of your Company Description.

COMPANY HISTORY, MILESTONES AND DEVELOPMENT TO DATE

Historical info

Founded in January 2006 by Scott Connors, ComputerEase began operation by providing software training at corporate customers' offices.

In March 2006, Susan Alexander became director of marketing. Ms. Alexander immediately began an extensive sales campaign, targeting 200 large companies in Scotland.

In August 2006, ComputerEase opened its software training centre at its present location in Edinburgh, enabling the company to significantly expand its offerings.

Identifies key milestone

Prior to opening the training centre, the company was limited in the services it could offer clients. The most lucrative business—continuing corporate contracts—was severely restricted, and no public seminars could be offered.

Nevertheless, in its first nine months of operation, the company conducted twenty-one on-site training programmes and secured ongoing training contracts with three primary target corporate customers.

Key milestones reached

When was your company founded?

How would you describe your current phase of development? (Seed? Start-up? Expanding? Stable? Retrenchment?)

What are some of the highlights of your company's history? What milestones have you reached so far?

QUICK**TIP**

Avoid Disclosing Sensitive Information

Be careful about putting highly proprietary or technical details in your plan, even if your reader has signed a non-disclosure agreement. You can present these details at a later stage of discussion.

4. Identify your product(s) or service(s)

Identify the specific types of products or services you sell. If you have a large product line or offer many services, you don't need to list each one separately. Instead, list the general categories.

For example, if you're opening a new gardening centre, you don't need to list all the specific plants and products you'll sell, just the general nature of your merchandise: 'a full line of plants for the home gardener, garden tools, planters and containers, plant food and chemicals, and a small selection of gardening books.'

When describing a product or service, provide just enough detail to give a clear picture of what it is or does. Too much detail makes this section cumbersome for your readers.

However, if you're seeking financing for a new type of product or service, particularly one that is not immediately understandable to your readers, provide more information. A brief explanation of what you'll be making or doing is appropriate here. Reserve detailed descriptions of production processes for the appendix of your business plan.

If you are changing the nature of your products or services, or plan to make changes in the future, describe the changes you anticipate. Explain why you plan to make the change—perhaps a new production method will result in cost savings—and how you expect your product/service line to differ over time.

SERVICES

ComputerEase offers training classes for users of all leading business software programmes. The company also devises custom training programmes for corporate clients. ComputerEase's classes are targeted primarily at the business-to-business market. Training classes are taught either on-site at the customers' offices or at ComputerEase's Training Centre in Edinburgh. To take full advantage of the company's resources, training classes for the general public are taught on Saturday at the company's Training Centre.

Range and nature of services provided

List your product(s) and/or service(s) and describe its function(s).

Product/Service	What It Does

What plans, if any, do you have to change your products or services in the future?

QUICK**TIP**

**Sniffing Out
Industry Info**

Researching industry trends enables you to provide facts supporting your claims for your company's potential success. Let's say you're opening a doggie day spa. This idea might raise investor eyebrows. You'll help overcome their scepticism by providing data showing the dramatic increase in spending on pets in recent years. Even more convincing are sales figures for pet clothing boutiques, doggie day care centres, and specialty pet-food shops.

5. Describe your industry

No business is an island. Every business, including yours, operates as part of a larger overall industry. Forces affecting your industry as a whole will inevitably affect your business, as well.

Every industry changes. Some changes come about because the customers for the products or services change. For instance, aging baby boomers provide new opportunities for industries serving retirees or the elderly. Other industry changes occur because of new technology, outsourcing or offshoring, or corporate mergers.

Make sure you address the major changes occurring in your industry. Indicate how you're prepared to take advantage of the opportunities presented and respond appropriately to any challenges you face.

Pay particular attention to your industry's recent economic health and rate of growth. When looking for financing, potential funding sources ask tougher questions if you're in a troubled or shrinking industry than if you're in a healthy, expanding one.

INDUSTRY DEVELOPMENTS AND TRENDS

ComputerEase is well positioned to take advantage of the significant opportunities presented by the rapidly expanding industry of computer-related business services. From 2001–2005, the industry grew in excess of 125%, compared to an overall GDP increase of approximately 29.5% during that period.

> Healthy industry growth

Computer software training is a relatively new industry, an outgrowth of the phenomenal expansion of computer use. The industry is still in a state of flux, with no market leaders, creating the opportunity for newer, smaller companies to succeed.

The key to success in the industry is to develop regionally known companies, as is currently the case with other business services such as accounting or employment services. These regionally-dominant training companies are able to earn revenues and build market share sufficient to sustain the high overhead due to the cost of equipment, skilled trainers, and materials.

> Strategic opportunity

The current lack of industry leaders represents an opportunity for ComputerEase to develop a strong presence and client base in the Edinburgh area.

In what industry (or industries) does your company operate? What types of businesses belong to this industry?

_____

_____

_____

Is your industry growing? What's the rate of growth?

_____

_____

_____

What trends in the industry provide you with opportunities?

_____

_____

_____

What challenges, if any, is your industry facing?

_____

_____

_____

How do you plan to capitalise on these opportunities and/or overcome these challenges?

_____

_____

_____

QUICK**TIP**

Invest in Yourself

Most lenders and investors want to see that the business owners have already made a significant personal financial investment in their own company. Many loan programmes require owners to contribute a certain per cent (often 20%) towards any funds sought. So make certain you highlight the amount of money—as well as the time and other resources —you've already committed to your company.

6. Explain your company's funding

The purpose of this section is to provide a brief explanation of your financing to date and, if you're seeking financing, to describe how much money you need and for what purposes. It's not meant to provide a total financial picture of your company. That will be seen later in your financial statements.

Don't go into specific details, such as your accounts receivable or payable, here. However, indicate any major sources of future funds already committed to you. For instance, if you have secured a three-year contract with a large customer that will generate significant annual income, this is a good place to highlight that fact.

If you're using your business plan to seek financing, indicate how much money you're looking for and how you plan to use the money you receive. You'll expand on this in your 'Sources and Use of Funds' worksheet on page 137.

FUNDING TO DATE AND FUNDS SOUGHT

Funding of the company to date has come from the personal savings of Mr. Connors. This has amounted to a £30,000 investment and £20,000 in loans. In addition, the company has received a £15,000 loan from Mr. Connors' family members. All other funding has come from the income generated by sales.

The company is now seeking £80,000 from outside investors. These funds will be used to open an additional Training Centre, hire trainers, add staff and expand marketing activities.

Indicates personal financial commitment of owner

Planned use of additional financing

How has the company been funded to date? How much have the company owners invested?

Has the company received funding from any other sources? If so, how much and on what terms?

What other major sources of funds has the company had?

How much money is the company seeking now and for what purposes?

Pulling It All Together: Company Description

A concise Company Description serves as a clear and convenient summary of the basic details of your company. Your Company Description provides readers with the facts they need to know about your company before delving deeper into your plan.

Draw from the information you provided in the worksheets in this step to complete this final worksheet.

What is the name and location of your company? (See worksheet on page 15.)

Who owns the company and what is its legal status? (See worksheet on page 17.)

What is your company's current phase of development, and what milestones have you reached to date? (See worksheet on page 19.)

What products and/or services do you offer? (See worksheet on page 21.)

What is the current health of your industry what are the key trends? (See worksheet on page 23.)

How has your company been funded to date? If you're looking for financing, how much money are you seeking and for what purposes? (See worksheet on page 25.)

3

Accomplishments

In this step you'll:

☐ 1. Identify your target market

☐ 2. Find the proof points that they exist and will spend their money with your company

☐ 3. Learn the basics of market research

Time-saving tools:

You'll complete this section more quickly if you have the following to hand:

☐ Internet connection for Government websites

☐ Lists of your product or service's strengths and weaknesses

Step 3:
Target Market

Your success rides on your ability to meet the needs and desires of your customers. In Step 3, identify these customers—not the *specific* people or businesses, but the *types* of customers you expect to serve. This is your target market.

Your goal is to assure your readers that:

- These customers do exist

- You know exactly who they are and what they want

- There are enough of them to support your business

- They're ready for what you have to offer and will actually buy

Paint a clear and detailed portrait of your customers—who they are, where they're located, how they think, why they buy, and what they want. This makes it easier to show how you plan to respond to their needs.

⚙ KEY TO SUCCESS
Creating a Credible Market Definition

A strong target market definition is:

Definable. It identifies the specific characteristics potential customers have in common.

Meaningful. These characteristics directly relate to purchasing decisions.

Sizable. The number of those potential customers is large enough to sustain your business.

Reachable. You can affordably and effectively market to them.

Strong target market definitions are based on observable characteristics, backed by data and research. This section outlines the kinds of information to include in a convincing target market description. See tips on collecting market research data on pages 32–33. If you have already done some market research, you'll complete this section more quickly.

1. Specify the geographic location of your target market

Provide details about the geographic location you're planning to serve. On the worksheet opposite, show where your customers live or where their businesses operate. Explain how other characteristics about the location affect your customers and your business.

If relevant to your business, include such information as:

* Neighbourhood, town, city, county, region, country, or international region

* Density of the area (urban, suburban, or rural)

* Climate (hot weather, cold weather, sunny, rainy, snowy)

* Traffic patterns (busy intersection, pedestrian area)

At this point, you are simply describing your target market geographic area, but your ultimate goal is to show the impact of its location on your business, if any.

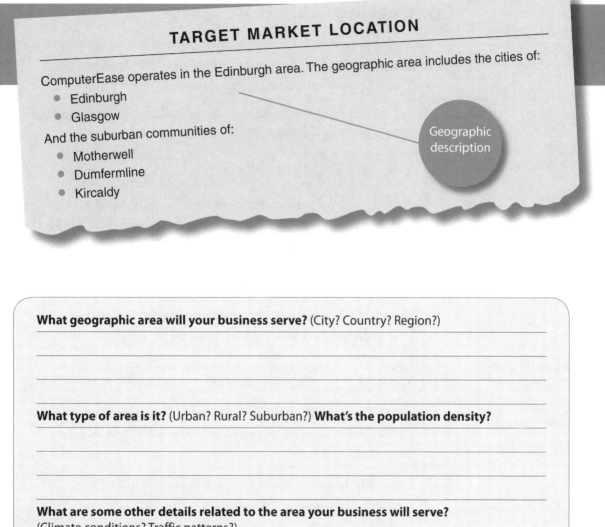

TARGET MARKET LOCATION

ComputerEase operates in the Edinburgh area. The geographic area includes the cities of:

- Edinburgh
- Glasgow

And the suburban communities of:

- Motherwell
- Dumfermline
- Kircaldy

Geographic description

What geographic area will your business serve? (City? Country? Region?)

What type of area is it? (Urban? Rural? Suburban?) **What's the population density?**

What are some other details related to the area your business will serve?
(Climate conditions? Traffic patterns?)

Conducting Market Research

Get to know your customers or potential customers. Try these tips to gain insight into your customers' needs and desires and to gather data that supports your assumptions about your target market:

- Talk to people or businesses that are, or could be, your customers. Ask them about what they want and need as related to your business.

- Conduct surveys and focus groups. These can be as informal as going to a mall and asking questions of consumers. If your budget allows, hire a professional market research firm to conduct interviews.

- Examine the media that your customers read, listen to, or view. Most media outlets, including newspapers, magazines, and radio and television stations, keep detailed demographic profiles of their audience and know what interests them.

- Check websites your customers visit, especially those in which they share their views.

- Check your local library. Your librarian can point you to online databases and print resources that provide data on your customers.

- Pay a visit (or several visits) to your competitors' places of business. Check out their websites. Work out what they do to attract and serve customers.

Get a Media Pack

Media outlets—magazines and newspapers, radio and TV stations—can be a good source of demographic and lifestyle info about their audiences. If you know your target customers are likely to read a particular magazine, call the publication and request an advertiser or media pack. Chances are, it will include demographic data you can use. Some publications put these kits right on their websites. (Follow the links for advertisers, often found in the 'About Us' section.)

Getting the Dirt On Your Market

Ever wonder why there seem to be three or four fast-food joints at the same intersection? Or why, all of a sudden, not one but three office-supply shops open in the same community?

The answer is that they all rely on similar statistics to choose locations. They look for particular factors: population density, characteristics of nearby residents (such as age, gender, income), and number and type of existing local businesses.

Big corporations hire consulting firms to compile these statistics. You've got an even bigger consulting group doing it for you—free! The British government, particularly the Office of National Statistics, compiles a great deal of data useful for businesses.

A few key websites for finding market data:
www.statistics.gov.uk: The Office of National Statistics online, for all current UK Census data. Use this for information on area breakdowns in terms of trade, income, geography and much more.

www.visitbritain.com: Website primarily aimed at tourists but which has ready information on geography and economic profiles.

http://www.hm-treasury.gov.uk/economic_data_and_tools/ forecast_for_the_uk_economy/data_forecasts_index.cfm Economic forecasts for the UK published by the Treasury.

QUICK**TIP**

Who's Your Customer?

Often, the person who purchases your product or service
is not the same one who uses
it. If you're selling to businesses, a purchasing department
or supervisor may be the decision maker. If you're selling to
consumers, a parent or spouse
may be the decision maker
and not the actual end user.
You need to understand the
needs and motivations of
both the buyer and the ultimate end user.

2. Describe the demographic characteristics of your target customers

Discuss the observable, factual characteristics of your target customers—traits such as age, income level, family size, gender, and ethnic group. If you are targeting businesses rather than consumers, these characteristics would include traits such as which industries they're in, the size of the companies, and their stage of development (new business, expanding, or shrinking). Look for *meaningful* characteristics that directly relate to your customers' decisions to purchase.

Say you're opening an elite hair salon in Cardiff. You identify your primary target customers as single, college-educated, professional women, aged 35–50, with annual income levels ranging from £80,000–£150,000. These demographic details indicate this group has more money to spend on high-priced salon services and the motivation to spend it.

Using the worksheet opposite, fill in details on your target market. The more specific your details, the more credible your market definition.

TARGET CUSTOMER CHARACTERISTICS

ComputerEase primarily targets large- and medium-sized businesses with high computer use. They have:

- More than fifty employees
- High employee turnover
- An expanding number of employees
- A high dependence on computers

They are in the following industries:

- Government
- Insurance
- Financial/Banking
- Accounting
- Colleges and Universities
- Engineering
- Hospitals and other medical facilities
- Airlines

Demographic and business-style characteristics

ComputerEase conducted a market research survey with a selection of targeted companies. It showed:

- 42% of these companies have a 'training' amount allotted in their current year's budget.
- 18% specifically have 'computer or software training' budgeted for the current year.
- 34% have purchased software training services in the last year.
- 66% indicated they would purchase more training than at present if better quality, more reliable training were available.

What are general, observable traits of your customers (especially those related to their likelihood of buying your product/service)?

Consumer (Age? Income range? Gender? Occupation? Marital status? Family size? Education level? Hobbies?)

Business (Industries? Years in business? Revenues? Number of employees? Specific business needs?)

3. Explain customer motivations and purchasing patterns

In addition to their observable demographic characteristics, highlight the less tangible, but no less real, factors influencing your customers' purchasing decisions. These include specific purchasing preferences, motivations based on how your customers view themselves, and how and when they actually buy.

When describing customer motivations, consider these questions:

- What concerns your customers most when making purchases? (Is it price? Quality? Convenience?)

- How quickly do they make their buying choices?

- Where do they usually buy their products or services?

- With what kinds of companies do they prefer to do business? (Large? Small? Socially responsible? Locally based?)

- How do your customers view themselves? (Do they see themselves as leading-edge? Technically savvy? Smart shoppers?)

When describing customer purchasing patterns, consider:

- Who makes the decision to purchase, if other than the end user?

- How often do they buy?

- How do they pay? (Cash? Credit? Purchase order? 30-, 60-, 90-day terms?)

Assess the organisational factors involved, especially if you are selling to other businesses. For example, large companies typically have formalised procurement systems, leading to slow purchasing decisions. This will affect the length of your sales cycle.

CUSTOMER MOTIVATIONS AND PURCHASING PATTERNS

In the corporations that ComputerEase targets, the decision to purchase computer software training is typically made by the human resources director or department. It often takes six to twelve months for a decision to be made. The critical issues influencing the decision are quality of the training, reliability, and responsiveness to specific corporate needs. Price is a consideration, but typically not the primary one.

Management personnel view themselves as responsible and professional. They prefer to deal with service companies that present a stable, professional image. They're often considerably influenced by the fact that similar companies already use the service or product.

Buying patterns

Customer motivations

Self-image issues

What factors most influence your customers' purchasing decisions?

Consumer (Price? Brand? Customer service? Features? Packaging? Return policy?)

Business (Price? Reputation/stability of service provider? Fast delivery?)

How do your customers view themselves?

Consumer (Trend-setter? Good house keeper?)

Business (Industry leader? Fiscally prudent?)

How do your customers actually purchase your products or services? Who makes the purchasing decision? Where and how frequently do they purchase?

Consumer

Business

QUICK**TIP**

QUICK**TIP**

Numbers, Numbers, Numbers

Your business plan will be more convincing with solid numbers describing the size of your target market. When your numbers come from a reliable source, numerical data shows you've done your homework.

4. Determine your market size

Is your market big enough to keep you in business? You want to make sure your pool of potential customers is large enough to sustain you. If you're looking for investors, you need to convince potential funders that your company can grow to a size that will make their investment profitable.

On the other hand, is your market so large you could never reach it affordably? If your market is too large, you probably have not defined its specific characteristics well enough to be able to design an effective and affordable marketing and sales process. Be realistic about the size of your market and your ability to serve it.

For some businesses, especially smaller ones, determining whether your market size is sufficient will be mostly a matter of intuition. But if yours is a bigger company, or if you're seeking investors, gather data to support your plan.

Be Specific

It's tempting to include just about everyone in the definition of your target market; after all, couldn't the whole world benefit from your product or service? Not only is this unrealistic, it makes it seem as if you haven't really zeroed in on who your real customers are—or could be. By detailing specific characteristics of your target market, you give readers a clearer view of your customers. Doing this will also save you time and money in future marketing efforts.

MARKET SIZE

Edinburgh and its surrounding communities make up a large and economically healthy area. According to census figures, Edinburgh has a population of approximately 675,000.

The business climate has been consistently strong due to Edinburgh's diverse economic base.

The Edinburgh Chamber of Commerce estimates that, of the more than 10,000 companies and institutions with more than fifty employees in Edinburgh, at least 2,500 are in the primary industries targeted by ComputerEase.

Also located in Edinburgh are:

- An international airport
- The regional processing centres for three major insurance companies
- The data processing centre for the national traffic police
- A university and four other colleges of higher education
- A major health trust

Market size data

Additional geographic information

What is the approximate size of your target market? (Include population of geographic area, if relevant, and total number of potential target customers.)

What other factors influence the size of the potential pool of customers?

5. Evaluate market trends

Change happens. You can't be a fortune-teller, but the most successful companies stay aware of trends that can affect their businesses. Such trends include: a growing (or shrinking) population, a hiring boom (or layoffs) in your area, a shift in the kinds of people or businesses populating the area, and new technologies. In this section, highlight the trends in your market, especially those which will have a positive impact on your business. Address trends that are occurring both in your geographic area and among the types of customers you serve.

Trade Associations

Trade associations are excellent sources of information about both the current customers in an industry and trends affecting that industry. Check with your industry's trade association for studies and forecasts they've published. You can find a list of trade associations at The Trade Association Forum website: **http://www.taforum.org/**.

MARKET TRENDS

The economic base of Edinburgh has been expanding. According to the Office of National Statistics, in the last four years the number of paid employees in the area has increased by over 50,000. A survey by *The Scotsman* has shown that 43% of larger companies intend to add employees in the next twenty-four months.

Promising trends

What is the rate of growth of your target market?

_____
_____
_____
_____
_____
_____
_____
_____
_____
_____

What changes are occurring in the makeup of the market? (Include changes in technology, the economy, and in social values and concerns.)

_____
_____
_____
_____
_____
_____
_____
_____
_____
_____

Pulling It All Together: Target Market

A key part of creating your plan, and running your business, is understanding your customers—who they are, what they want, how they make their purchases. This information helps you more successfully design your products or services, develop your marketing, and secure sales.

Now that you're well acquainted with your target customers and their needs, pull together the highlights of your target market definition. Complete the worksheet below, choosing the most important and relevant information you've compiled in Step 3. You can reorder the information to highlight the most compelling aspects of your target market.

Where is your target market located? (See worksheet on page 31.)
_____
_____

What are the characteristics of your target customers? (See worksheet on page 35.)
_____
_____

What motivates your customers to make purchases and what are their buying patterns? (See worksheet on page 37.)
_____
_____
_____

What is the size of your market? (See worksheet on page 39.)
_____
_____
_____

What are some key market trends? (See worksheet on page 41.)
_____
_____
_____

4

Accomplishments

In this step you'll:

- ☐ 1. Identify the types of competition you face
- ☐ 2. List your specific competitors
- ☐ 3. Determine market share distribution
- ☐ 4. Analyse the strength of your competitors
- ☐ 5. Highlight your competitive edge
- ☐ 6. Evaluate the barriers to entry and potential competition

Time-Saving Tools

You'll complete this section more quickly if you have any of the following handy:

- ☐ A list of major competitors
- ☐ Research on your competitors
- ☐ Industry or trade journal articles

Step 4:
The Competition

No matter what type of business you own or are planning to start, other companies want your customers. The fact that competition exists means you have tapped into a viable market with customers who want to buy the goods or services you have to sell. That's why other businesses, like yours, want to profit from them.

Even if you are trying to sell a new type of product, such as a groundbreaking new technology, expect competition. There may be no comparable product on the market, but there's probably something else that fits the market need. Take the photocopier, for instance. It was the first product of its kind but still faced competition. People were already duplicating documents using carbon paper and mimeograph machines.

The words 'we have no competition' in a business plan indicate to potential investors that a) an entrepreneur hasn't fully examined the realities of the business, and/or b) no market exists for the concept. If you're sure you have a market, you can be sure you have competition.

In the short term, understanding—and describing—your competition helps you present a stronger case to your business plan readers. In the long term, keeping an eye on your competition keeps you on your toes and helps you build and run a better business.

Just as important as *knowing* your competition is *learning* from it. Watch what your competitors are doing right and doing wrong. That will show you how to better serve your potential customers and uncover strategic opportunities in the market.

QUICK**TIP**

A strong competition section answers these questions:

- Who are your major competitors?

- On what basis do you compete? (Price? Convenience? Features? Service?)

- How do your offerings objectively compare to those of your competitors?

- How many new companies have entered the field in the past few years? Who are they?

- What barriers to entry make it difficult for new competitors to enter the market?

- What new competition might surface in the future?

1. Identify types of competition

What kinds of businesses contend with you for your customers' attention and money? Refer to *categories* of businesses here, rather than specific establishments. (You'll do that later.) For example, a clothing boutique might identify all similar boutiques within a ten-mile radius, *plus* well-known websites. An accountant might point to all other local accountants in town *as well as* popular accounting software programmes. List these categories of competition, along with the strengths and weaknesses of each, on the worksheet opposite.

Types of Competition

You face two types of competition: direct and indirect.

Direct Competition: Companies offering products or services much like yours that customers perceive as acceptable alternatives for example, Honda vs. Toyota or Burger King vs. McDonald's).

Indirect Competition: Companies offering products or services different from yours that meet the same or similar need. Customers can substitute your competitors' offerings for yours, for example, TV advertising vs. radio advertising or train travel vs. air travel.

When developing this section, always consider less obvious sources of competition that attract your customers' attention and money.

TYPES OF COMPETITION

Competing with ComputerEase to supply software training services to the target market (businesses making substantial use of computers and having more than fifty employees) are these categories of software training providers:

- Individual independent training consultants
- Local software training companies
- National training companies
- Software developers
- Community college classes
- Trainers from within the targeted companies themselves
- Online distance learning/training programmes

Describes the range of competitors

ComputerEase does not intend to compete with training provided by software developers. Such software is usually highly specialised and training is often included in the cost of the software itself. Community college classes are generally not competitive in the marketplace; classes are held in the evenings for at least ten weeks, conditions that do not meet business customers' needs.

Narrows the competitive field

List the types of businesses, not the specific companies, that compete with you. What are their strengths? What are their weaknesses?

Competition Type	Strengths	Weaknesses

QUICK**TIP**

Shop Your Competition

To collect valuable data and insights for your plan, spend time patronising your competition. What attracts customers to them? How were you treated? Were their products reasonably priced? Visit your competitors' websites. What features or attributes do they highlight? Get to know your competition through their customers' eyes.

2. Identify your specific competitors

Zero in on specific businesses that compete for your customers on a day-to-day basis (such as the boutique down the street or another neighbourhood accountant). Evaluate them in the same way you did your categories of competitors, based on how customers view them and how they operate.

Also note other attributes that may affect their ability to compete, such as:

- Do they have a well-known brand?
- Have they historically been the market leaders?
- Have they been growing?
- Are their marketing efforts focused specifically on your geographic target area?
- Do they have any strategic partnerships with other companies that give them marketing or operational advantages?
- Do they have any exclusive sales or distribution relationships?

Honestly evaluate your competitors. Resist the temptation to dismiss their products or services as inferior to yours. After all, there's a reason they're still in business.

Evaluating Your Competitors

Many factors beyond product quality and price come into play when evaluating competitors. Here are the two main categories of competitive factors:

Customer Perception Factors. Things customers can see. What product/service/company attributes make your competitors attractive or unattractive to your customers? These include: price, quality, customer service, and social consciousness.

Internal Operational Factors. Things customers can't see. What operational aspects put your competitors in a stronger or weaker position? Operational aspects include: labour costs, marketing budget and expertise, location, access to suppliers, and strategic partnerships.

Consider both types of factors when completing the worksheets on pages 47 and 49.

SPECIFIC COMPETITORS

Eight local businesses and four individuals in the Edinburgh area actively market their software training services. An unknown number of additional individual consultants provide such training on a less visible level.

Only one local company has developed a substantial presence with the target market: JMT Training. JMT has operated for more than six years and is the largest local software training company.

The individual independent consultants generally provide training for just one or two software programmes. Only one consultant, John Smith, has a meaningful corporate client base for his well-regarded spreadsheet training programmes.

Other Competition

Three major national software training companies periodically conduct classes in the Edinburgh area. Lesser-known national companies also occasionally provide such services, generally targeting recent purchasers of particular software. Online training is relatively new, with little or no market acceptance.

In-house training taught by employees of the targeted companies varies widely in content, form, and quality. Very few companies have 'trainers'; most training is provided on an ad hoc basis from supervisors and fellow workers. A conservative interpretation of ComputerEase survey results indicate that at least 20% of such training would be contracted out if satisfactory training could be obtained.

Available, but insignificant, training resources

Field narrowed to just two significant competitors

What specific businesses (local, national, worldwide, and online) do you consider to be your direct competition? List them here by name, along with their strengths, weaknesses, and other notable attributes.

Competitor	Strengths	Weaknesses	Other Attributes

QUICK**TIP**

QUICK**TIP**

No Market Leader? Lucky for You!

It's difficult to unseat companies that already control a significant share of a market. Want to introduce a new cola-flavored soft drink? It's not easy getting customers away from Coke or Pepsi. You'd have better luck launching an energy drink. Entering a field where market share is widely divided—without clear leaders—gives you a better chance of getting a piece of an emerging market.

3. Determine your competitors' market share

Some competitors are more important than others. In particular, companies commanding the largest share of customers' money—in other words, 'market share'—present the fiercest competition. Even though these companies may not necessarily provide the best products or most attentive customer service, they're going to be hard to beat. If you're opening a neighbourhood hardware shop, you're going to have to watch what's going on at B&Q and Homebase.

In this section, determine which companies command the largest portion of your market. These competitors are significant because they:

● Tend to define the standard features of a product or service

● Significantly influence customer perceptions of the product or service

● Usually have and spend the resources required to maintain their market share

● Can undercut prices to maintain market share

On the worksheet opposite, list your major competitors along with the percentage of the market each one commands (in revenues and/or units sold). Indicate whether their market share is increasing or decreasing. If yours is an existing business, indicate your market share.

Where to Find Market-Share Data

Trade associations, corporate annual reports, business publications, and independent research firms provide helpful sources of general data to use for your market share section. Many university libraries have business databases and print resources available. The Institute of Directors maintains a business library open to members, and any director is eligible to join: www.iod.com

MARKET SHARE DISTRIBUTION

The responses to a ComputerEase survey indicate that target companies currently conducting software training utilise providers as follows:

Current Total Market-Share Distribution for Business Software Training in Edinburgh

□	2%	Community College
□	8%	Software Developers
▨	14%	Local Training Companies
▨	14%	National Training Programs
▨	17%	Individual Contractors
■	45%	In-house

The lack of a dominant market leader offers the opportunity for new competitors to enter the market successfully

List your major competitors (general, specific, or both). Who controls what share (portion or percentage) of the market? Are these shares increasing or decreasing? Include yourself, if you currently control part of the market. Use actual data, if available. Otherwise, estimate market-share percentage.

YOUR BUSINESS:	Market Share	Increasing or Decreasing?

COMPETITORS:	Market Share	Increasing or Decreasing?

4. Determine competitive positions

In previous worksheets, you've identified your competitors' strengths, weaknesses, and market share. Now it's time to analyse and rank your competition based on those factors. This shows you understand the relative strength of your competition and helps you focus on the factors necessary to compete effectively.

On the worksheet below, rank the specific competitors you identified on page 51 from strongest to weakest and provide reasons for their market standing.

Rank your major competitors by name from strongest to weakest. Give the reason for each ranking.

Rank	Competitor	Reason for ranking

COMPETITIVE ANALYSIS

This is how ComputerEase ranks the strengths of its competitors:

1. JMT Training
2. John Smith, independent
3. In-house trainers
4. National training companies
5. Other local companies
6. Online training
7. Other independent contractors

Relative strengths and weaknesses highlighted

JMT is considered the strongest competitor due to its current client base, the personality and sales skills of its owner, Janice Tuffrey, and its potential to associate with national franchise training operations. However, JMT's current training staff and materials are of inconsistent quality, and current clients have expressed dissatisfaction with the lack of quality control. Moreover, JMT lacks skilled management of its financial affairs, resulting in insufficient capital for marketing and updating equipment. No other local companies have either the financial or personnel resources to adequately respond to a well-organised, sufficiently funded competitor.

Can benefit from competitor's strengths

John Smith has established a reputation as an effective trainer of spreadsheet programmes and has a loyal client base. However, he has expressed a lack of interest in expanding his operation by hiring additional trainers, and he has reached full or near-full capacity. ComputerEase has begun negotiating a strategic partnership with Smith to sell additional training to his current customers. No other independent contractor has a substantial client base or adequate resources to respond to new competition.

National training companies market their services through direct mail or telemarketers and have no local sales force. Their customer base is neither loyal nor particularly satisfied with the service.

The quality of in-house trainers varies widely. However, since these trainers are already on staff, there is little or no additional cost to the customer for using them.

5. Highlight your competitive edge

Every business needs some advantages over the competition to attract customers and stay in business. In this section, present yours.

Some typical types of competitive advantages are:

- Price

- Product features

- Convenience (closer to—or faster for—customer)

- Aggressive, effective marketing programme

- Choice of industries/types of customers served

- Well-known brand

- Exclusive relationships (distribution, suppliers)

- Operational efficiencies

It's also useful to show how your competitors' weaknesses become your company's strengths. Let's say the market leader in your industry is large and bureaucratic. If your company is small and nimble, explain how you are better able to respond to sudden changes in market demand. Does your competitor rely on old technology? Highlight your use of state-of-the-art tools that better serve your customers.

COMPETITIVE EDGE

ComputerEase's advantages over its competitors include:

- It's a local, as opposed to national, provider.
- It provides a local, in-person sales force solely dedicated to the corporate market.
- It offers a company-owned training centre with state-of-the-art computers and up-to-date business software.
- It offers ongoing technical support for corporate clients at no or low cost.
- It has coordinated, consistent marketing and sales programmes.
- Its status as an 'Authorised Training Centre' for major software publishers gives it credibility, joint programmes, and pre-release and steeply discounted software.
- Its management is business-oriented, rather than computer-oriented.
- Its staff consists of high-quality, professional trainers, rather than contract workers.

Why will your customers choose you over your competition? List your competitive advantages.

6. Evaluate barriers to entry and potential future competition

An important factor to consider is what obstacles, if any, prevent new competition from entering the market. You may be able to take on all your current competitors, but if you're successful, will a flock of new competitors suddenly appear?

As you consider potential future competitors, think about the obstacles they might need to overcome to enter your market. Common obstacles, called 'barriers to entry', include:

- Patents and trademarks

- High start-up costs

- Substantial, hard-to-find technical or industry expertise

- Market saturation

- Restrictive licensing requirements or regulations

Make a few well-founded predictions about the sources of your competition over the next five years or so. Consider:

- **New companies entering the market.** Good resources for predictions in this area include articles in industry publications or local media.

- **Existing companies expanding their product lines.** Look at companies in related fields and examine their websites for press releases about new product offerings. Once again, check industry media.

BARRIERS TO ENTRY AND FUTURE COMPETITION

It is relatively difficult for new competitors to enter the software training field. Substantial start-up costs are involved when purchasing or leasing equipment, and high-quality trainers are difficult to find. Moreover, software providers are becoming increasingly selective about which companies they will allow to serve as 'Authorised Training Companies'. These relationships are crucial in terms of receiving pre-release, below-cost copies of software, co-sponsoring product introduction events, and customer perception.

However, the long-term outlook for the industry points to nationally franchised local training companies and online 'distance learning'. These represent the most substantial threat. Recognising this evolution, ComputerEase plans to affiliate with the highest-quality national franchise or independent trainers association as soon as practical and potentially add its own distance learning training.

Highlighted as a ComputerEase advantage earlier

National companies present a major threat

List your potential future competitors.

What obstacles might new competition face in trying to enter your market? What are the barriers to entry?

Pulling It All Together: The Competition

To be an effective competitor, you have to understand what you're up against. Honestly evaluating your competition, their strengths as well as their weaknesses, arms you to survive. If you think you have *no* competition, think again. If you're filling a genuine market need, then there certainly are—or will be—other companies who want a piece of the action.

Synthesise the information you've gathered into a concise, convincing description of your competition, one that highlights your competitive advantages.

What types of businesses compete with you? (See worksheet on page 47.)

Who are your specific competitors? (See worksheet on page 49.)

What share (portion) of the market does each competitor control?
(See worksheet on page 51.)

How would you rank your competitors (in terms of market position)?
(See worksheet on page 52.)

What are your competitive advantages? (See worksheet on page 55.)

Who will your future competitors be, and what barriers to entry do they face?
(See worksheet on page 57.)

5

Accomplishments

In this step you'll:

- ☐ 1. Summarise your marketing message
- ☐ 2. Describe your marketing vehicles
- ☐ 3. Identify additional marketing and sales strategies
- ☐ 4. Describe your sales team

Time-Saving Tools

You'll complete this section more quickly if you have any of the following handy:

- ☐ Marketing collateral (brochures, advertisements, press releases)
- ☐ Marketing budget and/or expenses
- ☐ Information about your sales team
- ☐ Sales history (for an existing business)
- ☐ Sales forecasts

Step 5:
Marketing and Sales Plan

You know you have a good product or service, but can you convince customers to buy it? This is where your marketing and sales strategy comes in. It describes your plans for spreading the word about your product or service and selling to your customers.

Because your marketing and sales plan outlines your strategy for securing customers and sales, it's a critical key to your success. Investors and lenders want to see:

- A realistic, costed and cost-effective marketing approach to informing potential customers about your products or services and the benefits offered
- An effective sales force
- Appropriate sales techniques and methods

Marketing vs. Sales

Marketing and sales, while closely related, have very different functions.

Marketing activities make customers aware of your product or service and the benefits it offers. Marketing activities include advertising (print, radio, TV, Internet), producing collateral material (brochures, product information sheets), preparing company websites, doing public relations (press releases, events), attending trade show exhibitions, and offering free sample giveaways.

Sales activities are direct interactions with your potential customers to solicit and procure orders or to make an immediate sale. Sales activities include in-person sales at a customer's home or place of business, telemarketing, e-commerce, direct mail, online sales, or selling merchandise in person at a shop, trade show, or other event.

1. Summarise your marketing message

Every business sends a message in its marketing. To be most effective, base this message on the strategic position your company stakes out in the marketplace—the way you intend to distinguish yourself from your competitors. For instance, if you are competing on price, your message is 'low-price leader'. If you're competing on convenience, your message might be 'one-hour service'. Perhaps you are exploiting a particular niche in the market, such as 'lawyers specialising in estate planning' or 'software for architects'.

Such messages set you apart from the competition and help customers quickly decide if you present an appropriate option for their needs and buying priorities.

Words to Sell By

Some of the best company slogans focus on their customers' needs and desires rather than their product's attributes. Here are a few examples. Be cautious, however, when attempting this approach yourself; it takes an enormous marketing budget to make these indirect taglines memorable.

SLOGAN	COMPANY	MOTIVATION
Just Do It	Nike	Customers want to reach their fitness goals
Because You're Worth It	L'Oréal	Bolsters the customer's self-image
Where Do You Want to Go Today?	Microsoft	You can do anything on Microsoft software
It's Everywhere You Want to Be	Visa	Customers want the convenience and financial means to live the life they desire
Another World	NatWest	Banking is easier with this bank

MARKETING MESSAGE

ComputerEase's slogan, 'We speak your language', is designed to reassure its primary market: large corporate customers. The slogan implies both that the software training itself will be comprehensible and that ComputerEase understands the needs of the business customer. As a play on the word 'computerese', the name is designed to be memorable, with the added implication that the company makes dealing with computers easy.

ComputerEase prominently features its slogan, 'We speak your language', on all its marketing materials, on its company website, and at the bottom of email messages.

Marketing message and slogan

How do you position your company in the market? How do you want customers to think of your company? Summarise your message in fifty words or less.

Do you have a company tagline or slogan? Include it here.

QUICK**TIP**

A Good Fit?

Make sure your marketing approach, and the marketing vehicles you choose, are a good fit for the type and size of business you run. A small graphic design firm may be most successful spending its marketing budget by joining and attending local entrepreneur networking groups, while a shop may do better advertising in a local newspaper.

2. Describe your marketing vehicles

Once you have summarised what you want to tell potential customers, explain your plan for getting your company's name and marketing message out. Will you advertise? If so, where and how often? Exhibit at trade shows? If so, at which shows and how much will that cost?

Since every marketing vehicle costs money, carefully plan how you'll spend your marketing budget. Some options:

- Company website
- Product brochures
- Internet advertising
- Print media advertisements
- Broadcast media ads (radio, network and satellite TV)
- Promotional items (imprinted with your company name)
- Joining networking groups
- Public relations activities
- Direct mail

On the worksheet opposite, list the types of marketing vehicles you'll use. Also, indicate how often you plan to use them and how much it will cost. You'll use these figures later, in Step 9, when you prepare your financials.

A Magazine for Fenceposts?

While the mainstream press exposes your ad to more people, highly targeted publications reach those more likely to buy. If you sell specialised fences, you'll reach more potential customers advertising in a trade journal, like *FencePost* magazine or *World Fence News*, than in a general newspaper. There are trade publications for just about every industry or interest; locate them by using an Internet search engine.

MARKETING VEHICLES

Most of ComputerEase's marketing is done through face-to-face solicitation of human resource and training directors of large corporations. To support this effort, the company has developed quality printed sales materials (brochures and class descriptions). To stay in front of this market, the company also sponsors the annual dinner of the Edinburgh Association of Human Resource Directors and advertises in their quarterly magazine.

Additionally, the company maintains an ongoing direct mail programme. A schedule of ComputerEase's downtown classes is sent out every two months to the target audience. Currently 3,500 pieces are sent. ComputerEase purchases lists of human resource directors and another list of local subscribers to a leading computer magazine. All prior students are also included in the direct mail programme.

Marketing vehicles

What marketing vehicles will you use to deliver your message? (Advertising? Direct mail? Trade shows? Networking events?)

How frequently do you intend to use these marketing vehicles?

How much do you expect to spend on marketing each month? What is your annual marketing budget?

3. Identify any additional marketing and sales strategies

In addition to traditional advertising and marketing vehicles, many businesses work with other companies to promote their businesses and make sales. Some of these strategies include:

- **Strategic Partnerships**. Associating with another company to jointly promote each other's products or services or to have them promote your company as part of their offerings.

- **Licensing Agreements**. Licensing the rights to your product or service to another company, usually enabling them to sell your product or service under their name.

- **Distribution Agreements**. Arranging with another company to market and sell your product or service for you. Distributors often have their own sales force as well as warehouse and shipping facilities.

- **Using Wholesalers**. Wholesalers buy in bulk, then divide the goods into smaller quantities to sell to many retailers.

- **Working with Agents/Brokers**. These are individuals who sell your products or services, usually on a commission basis.

MARKETING AND SALES STRATEGIES

Marketing partnerships

ComputerEase partners with leading software publishers on many collaborative marketing activities. These include sharing the cost of cooperative advertisements placed in regional computer publications, sponsoring special events to introduce corporate clients to the publishers' new software, and sponsoring a trade show booth at the regional human resource directors' annual convention.

Strategic partnerships

Additionally, ComputerEase has agreements with two local computer hardware shops and four independent computer resellers to cross-promote each other's products and services. These shops and resellers include discount coupons for ComputerEase classes with every computer purchase they make.

What other marketing and sales strategies do you use, if any? (Include tactics such as co-op advertising, third-party distribution or licensing agreements, and other strategic partnerships.)

4. Describe your sales team

Your sales team provides your most important link to your customers— and to your profits. These staff members not only sell your product/service, they also have access to critical information about your customers' needs, desires, and buying habits.

The structure of your sales force reflects your sales methods: if you rely on face-to-face sales calls, you are likely to have salespeople on staff or use independent sales representatives. If you rely on telemarketing, you may employ part-time personnel or employ an outsource telemarketing company.

On the worksheet opposite, discuss the structure of your sales force. Detail whether you use:

- Full-time personnel
- Part-time personnel
- Independent sales representatives
- Employees of a different company

Explain how you pay your salespeople. Do they get straight salary? Straight commission? Base salary and commission? What percentage commission? Describe bonuses and other incentives you provide.

Types of Sales Reps

While sales teams can take many different forms, their responsibilities generally fall into one of three categories:

Internal Sales. They make sales while on the company premises. Telemarketers and retail shop sales staff are internal salespeople.

Field Sales. They visit customers to solicit orders and often nurture ongoing professional relationships with them. Pharmaceutical company agents who visit doctors and hospitals and employees who sell products in person to key clients are all examples of field salespeople.

Independent Sales Representatives. These are independent contractors (non-employees) who sell your products to a territory or to a range of customers. They may represent only your business; however, they often also represent products from a number of related companies at once.

SALES TEAM

Since ComputerEase's primary target market is large companies, most of its sales are made in face-to-face solicitations, primarily by the director for marketing, Susan Alexander, and also by company CEO Scott Connors. Both have extensive experience in selling to human resource and training directors—the primary decision makers in target companies. The average contract is projected at approximately £5,000.

The company also has two field sales representatives on staff, each paid £20 per hour, plus commission. Their primary responsibility is marketing ComputerEase training programmes to mid-size companies, a duty not handled by Alexander or Connors.

Additionally, all company personnel are considered members of the sales team. Susan Alexander is responsible for their sales training and supervision. The registrar, who takes phone registrations, is trained in phone manners and order solicitation, and she is given incentive gifts for registering targeted numbers of students for 'add-on' classes. Even the software trainers themselves participate in monthly sales training meetings. All employees receive financial bonuses if the company reaches overall sales goals.

Additional motivation to make sales

Who makes sales in your company? Do you have designated salespeople? If so, how many?

How are their jobs structured? (Internal sales? Field sales? Independent contractors?)

What are the highlights of your sales team's experience? How many combined years? Do any have a successful track record with products/services similar to yours?

How do you pay them? (Commission? Commission plus base? Salary? Bonuses? Incentives?)

How do you train them? What do you do to continually motivate them?

Pulling It All Together: Marketing and Sales Plan

To stay in business, you have to reach customers and secure sales. That is why this section of your plan is likely to be reviewed closely by prospective investors or lenders. In this section, potential funders want to see that your marketing and sales methods are appropriate for your business, and that your sales force is both large enough and well-enough trained to secure the sales levels necessary to sustain your business.

Synthesise all the marketing and sales information you've gathered into a clear, concise description of your marketing and sales plan.

What is your marketing message? (See worksheet on page 63.)

_____

_____

_____

_____

Which marketing vehicles will you use? (See worksheet on page 65.)

_____

_____

_____

_____

What other marketing and sales strategies will you employ? (See worksheet on page 67.)

_____

_____

_____

Who is on your sales team, and how is it structured? (See worksheet on page 69.)

_____

_____

_____

_____

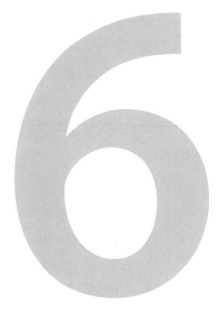

6

Accomplishments

In this step you'll:

☐ 1. Describe key operational factors
☐ 2. Highlight your corporate advantage
☐ 3. Find solutions to potential problems

Time-Saving Tools

You'll complete this section more quickly if you have any of the following handy:

☐ Maps of facilities
☐ Addresses of facilities
☐ Technological diagrams
☐ Work and production flow charts
☐ Operations-related financial records

Step 6:
Operations

How are you actually going to run your business? The Operations section of your business plan briefly describes how you execute the basic functions of your company: manufacturing or creating your product or service, keeping on top of inventory, and delivering your product/service to your customer.

Emphasise any operational aspects that give your company a competitive edge. If you've found a way to cut costs and increase profit margins by using innovative production methods or less expensive suppliers, highlight those aspects in your business plan.

Operational aspects of your business plan include:

- Location and facilities

- Production/manufacturing processes

- Equipment and technology

- Inventory management

- Cost controls and purchasing

- Quality control

- Customer service

How much detail you'll offer on each of these aspects depends on your type of business. For example, a catering company would focus on facilities and cost control; a limousine service would focus on equipment (vehicles) and perhaps technology (for dispatching). For more information on each of these components, see *Elements of an Operations Plan* on pages 74–75.

🔑 KEY TO SUCCESS

Your goal in this section is to show:

- You've thought through what it takes to make your company function.

- You are capable of managing those functions on a day-to-day basis.

- The reasons for any changes—and additional costs—in operations for an existing business (particularly if you're seeking funding).

Elements of an Operations Plan

- **Location and facilities.** The place you set up shop affects your ability to do business. Why did you choose this location and/or building? Proximity to your target market? Low rent or attractive lease terms? Easy access to transportation?

  How are the facilities arranged to make doing business easier? Describe the benefits of your location and facilities, *or*, if you're seeking funding to move to a new location, focus on the benefits of moving to a more appropriate place.

- **Production and quality control.** Every business has a production process. If you make a product, your process is the way you fabricate raw materials to create a new item; if yours is a service business, you'll have a method for designing and delivering your service to customers. Focus on issues such as your production methods, capacity, cost-saving procedures and the methods you use to ensure consistent quality control.

- **Inventory control.** If you are making or selling a product, how you manage inventory levels has a direct impact on your bottom line. You can have too much money invested in inventory that is just sitting around, or, conversely, not enough inventory to fill orders. Briefly describe the ways in which you manage your inventory levels to produce the highest profits.

- **Supply and distribution.** Who do you rely on to provide you with the goods coming into your company, and who do you rely on to help sell the goods coming out? Describe the relationships you have with key suppliers or distributors and wholesalers. Are your supply channels and distribution methods reliable? Do you have long-standing relationships and/or favorable credit terms with suppliers and distributors? Highlight the relationships that give your company added stability.

- **Order fulfillment and customer service.** Once you have produced your product or planned for your service, how do you get it to your customer? What are your packaging, shipping and warehousing systems? Do you have procedures for handling customer complaints or soliciting customer feedback? Show that you have an efficient system for fulfilling customers' orders and responding to their concerns.

- **Equipment and technology.** Perhaps you are using state-of-the-art or advanced equipment and technology to run your business or produce your product. If so, discuss ways this improves operational efficiency, saves money, and/or gives you a competitive edge.

- **Financial control systems.** Do you have procedures in place to make certain that financial matters are handled promptly and accurately? How are invoices sent out? How are your bills paid? Do you have a system to ensure that key managers are regularly reviewing financial information? A system for fraud prevention?

Keep It Simple

The Operations section of your business plan is *not* intended to be an operations manual. Rather, it is a brief overview demonstrating that you understand the nitty-gritty details that make your business work.

If yours is a very small business with simple operations (a home-based graphic design firm, for instance), you can omit this section altogether. However, you should then include a paragraph or two in your Company Description outlining your basic operations, such as what technology you use.

On the other hand, if yours is a new, expanding, or complicated business, go into more detail in your Operations section. Just remember: it's not necessary—or advisable—to provide a step-by-step guide to how your company works. Save that for an operations manual you use internally.

QUICK**TIP**

Are Your Operations Socially Responsible?

Socially responsible operations often lead to an enhanced bottom line and fewer problems with government agencies. You'll impress many investors and lenders by incorporating socially responsible practices into your operations plan. Do you have methods to reduce waste and excess energy use? Do you use recycled materials in production? Do your suppliers use sustainable business practices? Social responsibility is increasingly considered important by the customers, partners and affiliated businesses of a company. It is no longer a nice-to-have. It often pays to highlight those practices that show your commitment to the positive impact of your operations on the community and the environment.

1. Determine key operations elements

In this area, highlight the most important operational aspects of your business. Review the various operational aspects described in *Elements of an Operations Plan* on pages 74–75. Focus on those most central to your company's success. You don't have to include each element in your business plan, just the ones at your company's core. A catering company, for instance, could highlight its convenient and well-equipped commercial kitchen facilities, critical for enabling the company to handle large orders.

If yours is an unusual business—or, if you are seeking funding from a source not familiar with your industry—explain enough of the basic operations to enable your readers to understand how a company like yours functions.

KEY ELEMENTS OF OPERATIONS

A key element of ComputerEase's operations is its Corporate Training Centre, located at 43 Priory Street, Edinburgh. The Centre currently consists of twelve student computer stations, equipped with all the major business software programmes, an instructor's computer station and projection equipment, and state-of-the-art technology enabling the instructor to monitor exactly what each student is doing.

The Corporate Training Centre is vital because most of ComputerEase's corporate customers have limited, if any, extra computer facilities on their premises appropriate for conducting on-site corporate classes. Thus, ComputerEase can only grow to an adequate level of income by having well-equipped training facilities of its own to offer.

Describes a key operational factor

Explains reason for key factor's importance

List the operational factors most critical to your business and how you deal with them, then explain why they are important. You do not need to discuss every one of these factors here, only those key to your operations.

Your approach to:	Reason for Importance:
Location/Facilities:	
Production/Quality Control:	
Inventory Control:	
Supply/Distribution:	
Order Fulfillment/Customer Service:	
Equipment/Technology:	
Financial Control Systems:	
Other:	

2. Highlight your operational advantages

Here's where you can make your company—and your business plan—shine. Are you implementing, or devising, any operational efficiencies or innovations that give you an advantage over your competitors or increase profits? If so, be sure to highlight them here.

In this section, demonstrate how the operational choices you've made enhance your company's bottom line and give you an edge over your competition. For example, if a florist found a method of purchasing flowers directly from growers, rather than from wholesalers, he'd indicate how this improved his profit margins.

Explain any tradeoffs you've made by choosing a particular procedure, equipment or technology. The florist, for instance, might need to purchase additional refrigeration units, and incur additional costs, as a result of buying flowers directly, but could also show how those costs will be recouped in higher profits within a twelve-month period.

Which, if any, of your operational procedures or innovations enhance efficiencies, minimise costs, and/or maximise profits?

_____

_____

_____

_____

How do these compare with other companies in your industry?

_____

_____

How do they give you a competitive edge?

_____

_____

What, if any, are the cost/benefit tradeoffs of implementing these methods?

_____

_____

_____

OPERATIONAL ADVANTAGES

Having its own training classroom enables ComputerEase to enjoy higher profit margins than its competitors.

While maintaining a classroom incurs the additional costs of rent and equipment, training classes held at ComputerEase's Corporate Training Centre produce higher profit margins than classes conducted at customers' facilities ('on-site classes').

In comparison to classes held at ComputerEase's own classroom, on-site classes typically have fewer students per session, incur additional instructor and transportation costs, and increase wear and tear on equipment.

While ComputerEase charges higher fees per student for on-site classes, the market will not bear prices that truly absorb the increased costs.

Moreover, the potential customer base for Training Centre classes is substantially larger than that for on-site programmes. More businesses can afford to send employees to scheduled classes at ComputerEase's Corporate Training Centre—or have a class developed for them at the Centre—than can incur the costs and disruption of an on-site programme.

ComputerEase management chose to lease rather than purchase its Corporate Training Centre equipment and negotiated favorable lease terms with Wait's Computer Emporium, enabling the company to upgrade its computers every twelve months. This not only significantly reduced the initial capital outlay, which would have exceeded £50,000, but ensures that ComputerEase always has the latest technology for its students—a useful marketing, as well as educational, advantage.

With the funds now being sought, the company will open a second Corporate Training Centre in the city of Glasgow, where many of its corporate customers are located.

Drawbacks of alternate methods

Benefits include lower costs and larger customer base

Additional advantage of state-of-the-art technology

3. Address current—or potential— operational challenges

Most companies continually face changes and challenges in their operations, such as the need to update technology or equipment, find new facilities, or implement new processes or procedures. Perhaps you're developing your business plan to raise funds to deal with these needed changes. If so, you'll need to outline the problems you're currently experiencing, or the ones you anticipate in the near future, along with how you propose to address them.

In this section, describe any operational problems and potential solutions, addressing these questions:

● What operational issues currently reduce your competitiveness or profitability?

● What operational problems do you anticipate encountering in the near future?

● How do these problems affect your ability to do business or attract customers?

● What is your current plan for overcoming these problems?

● What are the costs associated with your solutions?

Innovative Operations

Are you creating a brand new product? If so, you may face additional operational hurdles. Is there a distribution system in place to get your goods to market? Are there adequate sources or supplies of raw materials? Have you figured out how to manufacture your product profitably?

In your business plan, briefly describe the issues facing you as an innovator and your planned solutions (without giving away trade secrets). Doing so shows that you are smart enough to realise there are added challenges when you're on the cutting edge.

OPERATIONAL CHALLENGES

A major part of the cost of the high quality corporate training offered by ComputerEase comes from the training materials provided to each student. Developing, writing, and continually updating training manuals for every software programme (materials are revised for each upgrade; their average lifespan is six to twelve months) costs £27 per student. To reduce waste, ComputerEase prints manuals just one day before each class begins, but doing so increases the per-unit cost.

The company recognised it had to substantially reduce materials costs. As new manuals are developed, they will be configured primarily for online, rather than print, delivery. All current training manuals will be available in digital form within eighteen months. This will, however, incur additional upfront costs in the development and deployment of the manuals for online access, and also require providing some tech support for students. However, making these changes will result in substantially increased profit margins within the next twelve months.

Current problem

Current approach to problem

Shows long-term solution to problem

What operational challenges currently face your company?

How are you dealing with these issues?

What operational challenges do you foresee in the future?

How much will it cost for you to adequately address these challenges?

Pulling It All Together: Operations

The Operations section of your business plan should not be overly detailed—save the specifics for your own internal operations manual. By describing the highlights of your operations, you show that you know how to make your company work on a day-to-day basis. This helps you to analyse any problems you're facing and think through solutions. And it increases confidence in your ability to structure and manage an efficient and profitable company.

Draw from the information you provided in the worksheets in this step to complete this final worksheet and develop the Operations section of your plan.

What are the key components of your operations structure? (See worksheet on page 77.)

_____

_____

_____

_____

In what ways do your operations structure and/or elements give you an advantage over your competition? (See worksheet on page 78.)

_____

_____

_____

_____

What are some operational challenges you're currently encountering or may face in the future? How do you plan to overcome those challenges? (See worksheet on page 81.)

_____

_____

_____

_____

7

Accomplishments

In this step you'll:

- ☐ 1. Highlight your key team members
- ☐ 2. Forecast future management needs
- ☐ 3. Describe your staffing structure
- ☐ 4. Identify members of your board of directors and advisory committee as well as any consultants

Time-Saving Tools

You'll complete this section more quickly if you have any of the following handy:

- ☐ CVs of key managers
- ☐ Organisational charts
- ☐ Salary and payroll numbers
- ☐ Biographies of board members, advisors, and consultants

Step 7:
Management Structure

Many readers of your business plan will turn to the Management section first. They want to know who's running the shop. Investors and lenders want assurance that the company is managed by competent leaders. In this section, you want to show that:

- The key members of your staff are qualified to run your business.

- You understand what additional staff, if any, is necessary.

- Your staffing levels and roles are appropriate and sufficient to achieve results.

- You've turned to qualified outside advisors when necessary.

🔑 KEY TO SUCCESS
Make Your Stars Shine

Do you have any well-known, highly accomplished people associated with your company? Have any of your key personnel had experience at well-regarded companies? If so, highlight these individuals prominently in your Management section and in your Executive Summary. Well-known names increase readers' confidence in your business plan.

How you prepare this section depends on how you're going to use your business plan. If you're developing your plan to raise money, focus primarily on the backgrounds of your management team. Summarise their relevant qualifications in a concise and objective style. If, on the other hand, you are creating a plan for internal use, concentrate instead on your staffing structure and the gaps in your team.

If yours is a very small business, and you are the key—or only—employee, you can omit this section. (However, be sure to emphasise your skills and experiencce in your Executive Summary.) To make your business seem more substantial, add the names and credentials of key advisors, such as your lawyer or accountant.

1. Highlight your key team members

This section describes the people who run your business. Develop brief summaries to explain their current roles and highlight their qualifications, past experience, education, and other characteristics, particularly as they relate to those roles. Your goal is to demonstrate you have brought together the right team to make your company successful.

Begin with the founder, usually viewed as the most important person in the company. Founders often serve as the top managers, exercising day-to-day control over business operations. Then list and briefly describe the other key members of your management team.

Some other key roles include:

- **Top decision makers:** Managing director, chief executive officer, division director

- **Operations:** Chief operating officer, plant or production manager

- **Technology:** Chief technology officer, MIS director

- **Marketing and sales:** Director of marketing, director of sales

- **Human resources:** HR director, training director

(Note: Founders often fill one or more of the roles listed above.)

If you are creating a business plan primarily to seek funding, limit the number of people you include to the five or six most critical to your long-term success.

As you describe each individual, explain:

- What is their role in the company?

- What past experience or education qualifies them for the job?

- What past successes have they had?

- What are their key professional and personal strengths?

- What (if any) is their personal financial investment in the company?

QUICK**TIP**

Building Tour Team

If yours is a young company, don't hire more people than absolutely necessary. Since your income is uncertain, it's better to start small and add staff—whether full-time or part-time—as your business grows. Instead, consider using outside consultants and contractors, even for relatively important tasks. You can outsource all types of responsibilities: sales, marketing, bookkeeping, human resources, and technology. As your revenues increase you can bring these tasks in house.

KEY TEAM MEMBERS

Scott Connors, managing director. Prior to founding ComputerEase, Scott Connors was the regional manager for Wait's Computer Emporium, a computer and electronics retailer with twenty-three shops in the North. Before that, he was a sales representative with IBM for five years.

Connors began his association with Wait's Computer Emporium as manager of the Edinburgh shop. In his first year, he increased sales by over 42%, in his second year by 39%. He was named 'Manager of the Year' for the Wait's chain.

Connors assumed the role of regional manager of the Wait's chain three years ago. He was responsible for the company's strategic development for Scotland and the North East. In that position, Connors conducted an evaluation of the potential of adding software training to augment the chain's computer hardware sales. This evaluation led Connors to believe that a substantial need for corporate software training existed but could not be met by an electronics retailer. Instead, a stand-alone operation should be formed. This was the concept behind ComputerEase.

Connors' association with Wait's Computer Emporium, coupled with his years at IBM, has given him an extensive background selling technology services and products to large corporations.

Connors owns 60% of the shares in ComputerEase and serves as Chairman and Treasurer of the Board of Directors.

Susan Alexander, director of marketing. Susan Alexander joined ComputerEase with primary responsibility for the company's marketing and sales activities.

Prior to joining ComputerEase, Alexander served as assistant marketing director for AlwaysHere Health Care Plan. Her responsibilities included making direct sales to human resource directors, developing marketing materials and campaigns, and supervising sales personnel. She held that position for seven years prior to joining ComputerEase. Alexander's experience marketing to the human resources community gives her the ideal background for ComputerEase, which sells its services primarily through human resources and training directors.

In previous relevant positions, Alexander was a sales representative for SpeakUp Dictation Equipment, where she sold technological equipment to corporations, and copy editor for the Catchem Advertising Agency.

Alexander owns 10% of the shares in ComputerEase.

Highlights demonstrated success

Related experience

Financial commitment to the company

Experience relates to several aspects of the business

**Describe the qualifications of your top-level management. List your key managers'
names, job responsibilities, relevant past experience, and other noteworthy attributes.**

Managing Director/CEO

_____
_____
_____

Key Management: Finance/Administration

_____
_____
_____

Key Management: Operations/Technology

_____
_____
_____

Key Management: Marketing/Sales

_____
_____
_____

Key Management: Human Resources/Personnel

_____
_____
_____

Key Management: Strategy/New Products/Research & Development

_____
_____
_____

2. Predict future management needs

New or changing companies usually have not yet filled all their key management positions. If you are looking for investors or lenders, it's likely that you're going to use some of the funds raised to hire additional leaders. In this section, summarise the roles you need filled and the desired qualifications of the people you hope to bring on board. Questions to consider include:

- What roles in the company will they be filling?

- What experience, qualifications, and education (if job-related) should they have?

- What other characteristics are you looking for in these individuals?

- How will these additional managers help round out your team?

Identify the types of individuals who will round out your team. For example, if your current team has strong marketing experience but less experience in managing money, adding someone with 'strong financial management experience' would be a priority in future management hires.

Use the worksheet opposite to summarise the desired qualifications of top team members you plan to hire in the next year or two. Their skills, experience, and personalities should complement those of other top managers and fill any perceived holes.

FUTURE MANAGEMENT NEEDS

Director, Training (to be selected). In the next year, ComputerEase will add a third key management position, director for training. The individual selected will have substantial experience running a training organisation, teaching others to train, and supervising training staff. This future director will possess outstanding training skills and have experience with computer software programmes, either in teaching or in developing such programmes. Ideally, he or she will have experience in developing training manuals or other training material.

> Balances out other team experience

What top management positions are you seeking to fill, or will you need to fill, in the near future? Describe the roles you anticipate and qualifications you'll be looking for in any future management employees. Omit this section if you do not anticipate hiring any additional key management in the next year or two.

1. Key Management to Be Hired

2. Key Management to Be Hired

3. Key Management to Be Hired

3. Describe your staffing structure

Describe the composition of the rest of your staff, the people who carry out the day-to-day work of your company. There's no need to provide the name and qualifications of each individual. Instead, present a general summary of your staffing situation, focusing on job roles, responsibilities, and staff costs. For example, a fashion boutique might have three salespeople making £10 per hour, plus commission, while a restaurant might include ten part-time waiters, paid a combined £110,000 a year, plus tips.

Use the worksheet opposite to describe the makeup of your staff. Also indicate any expected changes to your staff composition or staffing levels, such as adding additional employees, or plans to outsource responsibilities to independent contractors or consultants.

Social Responsibility Leads to Healthy Bottom Lines

Social responsibility encompasses a company's treatment of its employees along with the values exemplified and communicated by the corporate culture. Do you compensate your employees fairly? Do you provide, or at least contribute to, an adequate benefits package? Is your business environment free of racism, sexism, ageism, and any other 'isms' that would make it an uncomfortable place to work? While you don't need to dwell on this in your business plan, creating a fair and ethical work environment pays off. It translates into increased worker loyalty and productivity, leading to reduced staff turnover and training costs, as well as enhanced company image. These, in turn, can lead to greater customer loyalty and higher profits, as well as the satisfaction of knowing you've created a great place to work.

STAFF STRUCTURE

In addition to the two primary managers now on staff and a director for training to be hired, ComputerEase currently employs two permanent staff members. Additionally, the company contracts with training course leaders as needed, but they serve as independent contractors.

One of the two staff members serves as receptionist, customer service representative, class registrar, and mail handler. The other staff member also handles customer service, as well as dealing with tech support calls and maintaining the hardware and software for ComputerEase's classroom. Both make sales calls to individuals expressing interest in the company's classes (through ComputerEase's website or other leads). Each is paid £19 per hour.

As ComputerEase's course load increases, the company will hire part-time training instructors rather than relying solely on outside contractors. This will reduce costs, but as importantly, will ensure greater consistency in the quality of the company's offerings.

Staff to be hired in the future

What are the jobs of employees on your staff? List them here, along with the number of people who fill those roles, and their pay rate/range.

Job Role	Number of employees in that role	Pay Rate/Range

What staff will you add in the near future?

4. Identify your board members, advisors and consultants

It is often a good idea—and sometimes a legal necessity—to look outside your company for additional guidance and advice. If you have formal outside relationships, such as with the members of a board of directors, include the names and brief biographies of members in your business plan. For informal relationships, such as those with advisory committees or consultants, include information about them if they add credibility or stature to your company.

Some key outside advisors include:

Board of directors. Boards of directors typically have legal responsibility for a company. In start-ups, this may consist of only one person: the founder. In larger companies or companies with investors, the board usually consists of individuals with a financial stake in the company and, possibly, additional members knowledgeable about the industry. Venture capitalists generally require board membership as a condition of their investment.

Non-executive directors. Non-executive directors do not have legal responsibility for a company. Thus, it is possible to identify a range of individuals whose ongoing expertise and advice you'd like to have for your company. Non-executive directorships can be very informal, and may meet infrequently, but they give you a way to ask people you respect to assist you in building your company.

Consultants and other professionals. Almost all new and expanding businesses rely on consultants to provide critical guidance and professional services. Include these in your plan *only* if they play a key role or if their names will add luster to your business plan. Such consultants include:

- Lawyers
- Accountants
- Management consultants
- Marketing consultants
- Industry specialists
- Technology advisors

BOARD MEMBERS, ADVISORS, AND CONSULTANTS

BOARD OF DIRECTORS

Scott Connors is the Chairman of the Board and Treasurer.

Cathy Dobbs, the company's lawyer (and founder of the firm Dobbs, Kaye, and Babbitt) serves as Secretary.

The position of Vice Chairman has been reserved for an outside investor.

Board consists of founder and outside professional advisor

NON-EXECUTIVE DIRECTORS

An informal advisory committee provides guidance to the officers and staff of ComputerEase. The committee meets quarterly, and members of the committee are available as resources to the company on an ongoing basis. The members represent professionals from industries directly related to ComputerEase's mission and target market.

Members of the committee:

Mary Major, Director of Human Resources, RockSolid Insurance Company

Brian Luce, Director of Training, Scottish National Bank

Alex Arthur, Marketing Director, SANE Software

Dr A.A. Arnold, Professor of Instructional Media, Edinburgh University

How committee serves the company

CONSULTANT

A.A. Arnold, Ph.D. Dr A.A. Arnold, Professor of Instructional Media at Edinburgh University, serves the company as a consultant in the conception and development of training manuals. A specialist in the design of instructional materials, Dr Arnold received his Ph.D. in Education with an emphasis on interactive computer-aided training. Currently, Dr Arnold designs training programmes for industry in addition to holding his position at the University.

Outside consultant gives added credibility

Do you have a board of directors? If so, who are the members? List them here, along with brief biographies, including their professional expertise, financial stake, and compensation (if any).

If you have non-executive directors, who are they? List them here, along with their professional affiliation, expertise, value to your company, and compensation (if any).

Do you use consultants? List them here, including the names of their firms, areas of expertise, and the ways in which they serve your company.

Pulling It All Together: Management Structure

Use the worksheet below to prepare the management section of your plan. If yours is a large company, add an organisation chart to illustrate how your company is structured.

Conclusion

The success of your business depends on the people who run it. It takes capable people—with appropriate experience and abilities—to build and run a thriving company. Thus, it is no surprise that lenders and investors often turn first to the Management section of a business plan. They want to make certain the people in charge have the background necessary to manage the company.

Who are the key people on your management team? (See worksheet on page 89.)

What management positions do you need to fill in the near future? (See worksheet on page 91.)

What is the make up of the rest of your staff? (See worksheet on page 93.)

Who are the members of your board of directors and non-execs, and who are your consultants? (See worksheet on page 95.)

8

Accomplishments

In this step you'll:

☐ 1. Define your long-term goals

☐ 2. Establish future milestones

☐ 3. Assess the risks

☐ 4. Explore exit options

Time-Saving Tools

You'll complete this section more quickly if you have any of the following handy:

☐ Existing plans for company development

☐ Calendar of planned product releases or expansion activities

Step 8:
Future Development

Since a business plan is a road map for your company, you—and those who review your plan—need a clear sense of your ultimate destination. In this section, you'll outline your long-term goals, indicating the milestones you plan to reach along the way. By developing specific objectives, you'll have signposts to measure progress as you go.

If you're seeking investors for your business, this section will be of particular interest to them. When they invest money in your company, they want to assess exactly how much they might gain eventually, and how big your company might become. Only then can they understand the potential return on their investment.

It's also important, both to you and your investors, to spell out what might ultimately become of the company. How will you (and any investors) get your investments—and rewards—out of the company in the long term? Even if you're just starting your business, you'll find that considering possible exit strategies changes the way you think about your company and gives you a framework for business planning.

Finally, don't be afraid to look at the risks involved in your business. An honest assessment of risk isn't likely to frighten experienced investors or lenders. They understand that all ventures involve some risk; they'll respect the fact that you understand and anticipate the risks involved.

🔑 KEY TO SUCCESS
Tailor Your Plans to Your Needs

What you include in this section depends on the purpose of your business plan, especially if you are seeking funding. If you're looking for funds to finance growth, this is the place to share your vision. If, on the other hand, you're looking for money to deal with financial difficulties, use this section to explain the changes you'll be making to improve your company's health.

QUICK**TIP**

If yours is a small business, make sure your business goals fit your personal goals. If you want to be home by 4 p.m. and take long vacations, it's unrealistic to set the goal of building a very large company.

1. Define your long-term goals

What do you expect your company to look like in one year? Five years? Ten years? In this section, describe your long-term vision and plans. Be as specific as you can, focusing on issues such as:

- Turnover levels

- Profit levels/margins

- Number of employees

- Number of locations

- Number of product(s)/product lines

- Market share

For example, a small accounting office might have the goal of securing twenty new corporate clients in the next year, adding two additional accountants and a bookkeeping service over the next three years, and opening a second location within the next five years.

Qualitative versus Quantitative Goals

If you have not yet determined specific, quantitative goals—the kind with numbers attached—include any other goals you have for your company. Even though these may be less specific than sales or profit goals, they still give an indication of the direction you plan for your business. Such qualitative goals include: dominating a niche market, penetrating a new market, being an industry innovator, or becoming the recognised quality leader.

LONG-TERM GOALS

Intends to become a local market leader

ComputerEase plans to grow steadily over the next five years, becoming the premier provider of software training to large and medium-sized businesses in Scotland. It will capture a market share of at least 50% of all corporate software training (in terms of revenues) in the area. Within ten years, the company plans to have expanded throughout Edinburgh, Glasgow, Newcastle and Aberdeen, with offices in five to ten locations, having captured at least one-third of the share of the corporate software training market in the region.

Describe what your company will look like in the future. Be specific about sales levels, products, profit levels, and numbers of employees and locations.

What are the specific goals you have for your company in the next year?

What will your company achieve in the next three to five years?

What will your business look like in ten years?

2. Establish future milestones

How will you know that you are making progress toward your long-term goals? Milestones will help you measure how far you've come.

Your milestones should be described in specific numerical terms so you'll know if you're making sufficient progress toward your goals. The accounting office, for instance, could set as a future milestone reaching £650,000 in revenue by the end of the second year, or have a goal of adding five new clients within the next three years.

Outlining your milestones also serves as a step-by-step guide, showing how you intend to carry out your long-term business development plans. If, for instance, your goal is to reach sales of £3 million by year five, indicate how much you'll need in sales by years two, three, and four. Then, indicate the strategies you'll use to get to those levels. Will you add marketing staff? Start a direct mail campaign? Add locations or product lines?

A milestone list allows you and your investors to see what you plan to accomplish, and it sets out clear objectives. These objectives are an essential part of your business plan.

What Milestones Have You Reached?

Instill confidence in your future prospects by highlighting your past achievements, the milestones you've already reached with your business. Include these past milestones in your Company Description (see page 19). But don't be afraid to repeat them here if they demonstrate that you're likely to reach your future goals, as well. For example, if you've already established strategic partnerships with three industry leaders, that's a good indication you can forge three more as you've indicated in your future milestone list.

FUTURE MILESTONES AND DEVELOPMENT STRATEGY

First year milestone

To reach the long-term goal of becoming one of the dominant companies in corporate software training in the North, ComputerEase will add training classrooms and locations each year for the next three years.

The first priority is to open the company's second Corporate Training Centre in the city of Glasgow within a year. Many large- and medium-sized businesses are located in the immediate vicinity of Glasgow, and the location can serve both as an additional training classroom and as a base of additional marketing activities. One new full-time marketing employee will be added to work out of that location.

Describes short-term strategies necessary to meet longer-term goals

In each of the following two years, ComputerEase plans on opening at least one additional company-run Corporate Training Centre, concentrating on cities within a three-hour drive of Edinburgh that have a substantial number of large- and medium-sized corporations.

Additionally, within twenty-four months, ComputerEase will launch its online training programme. To do so, a consulting firm specialising in the development of such online training programming must be hired within the next six to nine months.

By year three, ComputerEase management will assess future options for growth. Likely scenarios include the addition of more company-run Corporate Training Centres or the possibility of franchising the operation.

Long-term expansion strategies

List the specific accomplishments you'll achieve on the way to your long-term goals. Give numerical objectives—sales and profit figures, number of customers, employees, and locations—and target dates.

Milestone	Level Achieved	Target Date

What specific steps will you take to reach those milestones?

3. Assess the risks

Running a business entails a measure of risk. Even a company with highly qualified management and well-conceived strategies might be affected by outside events.

Some types of risk any company—including yours—faces include:

- **Competitive risk.** Competitors may drive down prices, market their product or service more aggressively, or substantially enhance their offerings; new competitors may enter the field.

- **Market risk.** The economic health, needs, or desires of the target market may change.

- **Operational risk**. Critical aspects of your operations may change—suppliers may go out of business; equipment or technology may change.

- **Financial risk.** The cost of materials, energy, or labour may rise substantially.

- **Execution risk.** You may not be able to achieve the results planned in the time predicted, or you may not be able to manage your growth.

- **Economic risk.** The health of the overall economy may change, or specific financial factors, such as interest rates, may have a negative effect.

In this section, spell out the risks you're most likely to face, along with the steps you'll take to reduce those risks. If you're looking for funding, show investors or lenders that you're realistic about the challenges you could face.

RISK ASSESSMENT

The biggest risk facing ComputerEase is from new competitors entering the market from outside Edinburgh. It is highly likely that existing franchised software training companies from other parts of the UK will open franchises in this region. Since these national companies offer financing to their franchisees, the major barrier to entry—the cost of establishing a training centre—can be overcome. If the franchisee is highly capable, this represents the greatest risk to ComputerEase.

To prepare for this eventuality, it is critical that ComputerEase quickly and aggressively increase its market share in the region. Corporate customers are slow to change established vendors, and the company anticipates that they will be able to retain a high percentage of existing customers even in the face of new competitors. Moreover, ComputerEase management remains open to the possibility of a merger or other agreement with a national company if that appears to be a better financial option.

The second greatest risk is that significant changes will occur in the market. ComputerEase is highly dependent on the corporate market. Companies leaving the area, downsizing, or reducing their training budget would have a direct negative effect on ComputerEase revenues.

To counteract this, the company will increase its marketing of Saturday classes—and add evening classes—for consumers. In the event of layoffs, individuals will need to take classes to improve their skills, and this will provide some balance to the corporate market.

Identifies risks from potential competition

Strategy for reducing risk

What are the potential risks facing your company? List them here, along with your plans to minimise them.

Potential Risks	Plan to Reduce Risk

4. Explore exit strategies

If you're just starting your business, it's hard to imagine what might eventually become of your company. But thinking through scenarios of what might ultimately happen to your business is helpful to you, and it's absolutely essential for investors.

An exit strategy gives focus to how you'll build your business. If you'd eventually like to sell your business, you're going to plan your business quite differently than if you'd like to hand it down to your children or have it go public on a stock exchange. See page 108 for more on exit plans.

If there's more than one partner or principal in the business, having a clear exit strategy reduces the friction that can come from having unspoken assumptions. One founder may dream of building a company worth millions and selling it in a few years, while the other may hope to build a modest company they can run together for many years. Sitting down and clarifying an exit strategy puts both on the same track.

An exit plan is absolutely critical if you're looking for investors. After all, they want to know how they will get their money back. Once you've built up the value of your business, how will that value be converted to cash or easily traded stock?

THE EXIT PLAN

By establishing itself as a regional market leader, ComputerEase will become a likely target for acquisition by a national software training company or other national for-profit educational institution. For-profit education companies are among the fastest growing firms in the UK, and they regularly acquire existing training schools as a method of achieving their growth.

Moreover, as other software training companies have demonstrated, the ComputerEase concept lends itself well to franchising. Franchising would produce additional revenue streams to the company from the franchisees, both from franchise fees and through the purchase of materials and staff training. If the decision is made to franchise, venture capital investment will be sought. Current investors could choose to liquidate their holdings in ComputerEase at that time or convert their holdings to stock in the franchise operation.

Describe the likely exit strategies for your company. If you're seeking investors, concentrate on strategies enabling you and investors to convert the value of your company to cash or easily traded stock.

Exit Plan Options

OPTION	DESCRIPTION	BENEFITS	DRAWBACKS
Go public	Sell stock in the company on a public stock exchange	The stock easily converts to cash; liquidity	Must be a large company; approx. £25 to £50 million; highly regulated
Acquisition	Another company buys yours	Investors receive cash and/or stock	Must be a good fit for the existing company; company must have clear value
Sale	Individuals buy the company	Investors get cash	Must find a willing buyer; company must have clear value
Merger	Join with an existing company	Investors may receive stock in the new company or some cash	Usually little or no cash; stock may not be easily traded
Buy-Out	One or more current shareholders buy out the interest of another	Sellers get cash	Buyer must have sufficient cash; negotiations often contentious
Franchise	Replicate concept by licensing rights to others	Receive cash; franchisees finance expansion	Concept must be appropriate; legally complicated
Hand-Down	Give company to the next generation	Stays in family	Family tensions; little or no cash; tax implications
Close	End operations	Relatively easy; sense of closure	No financial reward; possible sense of loss

What Is ROI?

One of the most important factors investors consider when deciding whether to finance a company is the potential ROI, or Return on Investment.

ROI is the amount of money an investor gains in return for their investment. ROI is usually expressed as an annual percentage of the total investment. This figure makes it possible to quickly compare different financial opportunities, such as investing in a specific company versus investing in the stock market. Investors are looking for the largest return on their money, so the higher the ROI, the better.

The basic factors determining an investment's ROI include:

- All financial costs—initial investment and any follow-on investments
- All financial gains—including both the increase in funds (if any) from the investment and the return of the investors' money
- Time period—how long it takes to realise these gains

There may also be non-financial benefits of an investment that figure in an investor's decision, such as the satisfaction to be gained from participating in a young company's growth.

Let's say an investor is considering investing in one of two companies:

Company A: A £50,000 investment is projected to return a total of £100,000 to the investor in 2 years.

Company B: A £150,000 investment is projected to return a total of £300,000 to the investor in 4 years.

In both scenarios, the investor doubles their money. So which is the better investment?

An investment in Company B nets the investor a larger monetary gain: £150,000 versus only £50,000 in Company A. *But*, due to the length of time required before the investment in Company B pays off, the simple ROI in Company A is actually higher:

- Company A: 200% return in 2 years or 100% ROI per year
- Company B: 200% return in 4 years or 50% ROI per year

Pulling It All Together: Future Development

The Development section of your business plan shows you have given careful thought to how your business will grow over time. Present your readers with a clear vision of your future, along with a realistic strategy for getting there. Be sure your plan incorporates well-defined goals, specific milestones, and an honest assessment of risk. And be certain to include an exit plan; demonstrate how you and your investors can eventually recover the investment you've put into your company and convert any increase in value into cash.

What is your long-term goal for your company's future? (See worksheet on page 101.)

_____
_____
_____
_____
_____

What milestones will you reach along the way? (See worksheet on page 103.)

_____
_____
_____
_____

What are the risks involved and how will you minimise those risks? (See worksheet on page 105.)

_____
_____
_____
_____

What are the possible exit options? (See worksheet on page 107.)

_____
_____
_____

Accomplishments

In this step you'll:

- ☐ 1. Produce your Income Statement
- ☐ 2. Develop your Cash-Flow Projection
- ☐ 3. Generate your Balance Sheet
- ☐ 4. Show your Sources and Use of Funds
- ☐ 5. Consider preparing additional supporting financial statements

Time-Saving Tools

You'll complete this section more quickly if you have any of the following handy:

- ☐ Current and past financial records
- ☐ Historical sales figures
- ☐ Projected costs
- ☐ Payroll numbers
- ☐ Any past loan documents
- ☐ Company tax returns for past years (for an existing company)
- ☐ Sales projections, marketing budget, staffing budget

Step 9:
Financials

People in business fall into one of two categories: those who fear dealing with numbers and those who are fascinated by them. If you're in the first category, the prospect of completing all your financial statements can be intimidating.

Moreover, if you're using your business plan to seek funding, it's daunting to know that investors or lenders often turn to the financials first. That's because your financials give a clear picture of how you earn and spend your money and how big you expect your company to become.

Take heart: numbers are not magical, mysterious, or menacing. They merely reflect the decisions you've made in planning or running your business. If you run ads every week in your local newspaper, there's a number associated with that. If you hire a person to help with shipping, there's a number associated with that, too.

Of course, if yours is an existing—rather than a new—company, you may already have many of these financial documents, or the basis for creating them. Examine your past financial performance and expenses when putting together your future projections and include historical numbers in your business plan.

⚙ KEY TO SUCCESS

Overcoming Finance-Phobia

If you shy away from dealing with numbers, it's easy to get into financial trouble. Learn to pay attention to your ongoing financial situation. It will help you avoid unpleasant surprises. Even if you leave the number-crunching, bill paying, and financial data entry to someone else, familiarise yourself with how to read and understand your financial statements. They'll help you make better business decisions and retain more control over your operations.

The Most Important Financial Statements

The four most important financial statements to include in your business plan are:

1. **Income Statement.** Shows whether your business is profitable (this is also called a Profit & Loss statement or 'P&L').

2. **Cash-Flow Projection.** Indicates whether you'll have enough money to pay your bills.

3. **Balance Sheet.** Shows the value of your company—your total assets and liabilities.

And, if you're seeking financing:

4. **Sources and Use of Funds.** Explains where the money you need to run your business will come from (including your own pocket) and the major ways you intend to use it.

These four financial statements act as a summary of your entire financial picture, and they may be the only financial statements you need to include with your business plan, especially if yours is a simple business.

However, before preparing these four major financial statements, you'll find it helpful to produce the following:

- **Sales Projections**. Estimates your levels of sales and revenues in specific time periods.

- **Marketing Budget:** Details how much money you'll spend on all your marketing activities: advertising, trade shows, sales materials, and so on.

- **Staffing Budget:** Outlines your staffing levels, staff positions, and costs.

See page 138 for more information.

Time Periods to Cover

Some investors or lenders will tell you the time periods they want your financial statements to cover. If not, here are typical guidelines for:

New businesses: One to three years. First year, monthly projections; years two and three, quarterly projections.

Existing businesses: Same as for new businesses *plus* historical financial records from the past three to five years.

Businesses seeking venture capital: Five-year projections. First one to two years, monthly; years two and three, quarterly; years four and five, annual projections.

Additional Financials

Depending on the nature of your business (and the demands of your investors or lenders), there are a number of additional financial documents you can choose to include with your business plan. These include:

- **Break-Even Analysis.** Calculates how much you need to make in sales each month before you begin to make a profit.

- **Capital Expenditures.** Details purchases of tangible property, such as facilities, land, equipment, vehicles, and computers. Such purchases have different tax and accounting implications than other expenses.

- **Inventory.** Details the amount you spend or have tied up in inventory.

- **Professional Services Budget.** For a company that depends heavily on outsourced professionals, including independent contractors, consultants, lawyers, and accountants.

Since most businesses do not need to include these financial statements with their business plans, they are not included here.

QUICK**TIP**

Hire a Professional

Every business benefits by having access to the services of an accountant or bookkeeper, especially in the early stages. Among their many valuable services, they'll help:

- Set up your books

- Assist you in understanding financial terms and legal requirements

- Provide valuable advice on billing, payment, and payroll procedures

- Advise you on tax-saving strategies

- Assist with the financial components of your business plan

1. Produce your Income Statement

Your Income Statement, also referred to as a Profit and Loss (P&L) statement, is the most widely relied upon of your financial statements. It summarises the amount of money taken in and the amount of money spent over a designated period of time. This summary of revenue and expenditures reveals whether your company is profitable. It is read from top to bottom, with the first line showing total overall sales. Each subsequent line shows expenses that are deducted from your income until you get to the number at the end representing your profit or loss: your 'bottom line'.

To prepare your Income Statement, gather detailed information about your sales and expenses. Feel free to change the terms/language on the specific lines—especially in the expenses section—to mirror the categories you use to maintain your own accounts. Using the worksheet on pages 122–123, compile your pro forma (projected) Income Statements on a month-by-month basis. Use the same line items to produce annual or quarterly Income Statements. If yours is an existing business, use the same form for your historical Income Statements.

Your Income Statement provides the quickest overview of your company's profitability. Investors and lenders are naturally interested to know when you're going to be profitable and how much money you'll be making.

In addition to a month-by-month Income Statement for the current or coming year, include projections for the next few years. On the pages that follow are two sample Income Statements: a month-by-month Income Statement for the fictional company ComputerEase's first year in business (pages 118–119) and a three-year projection compiled on an annual basis (page 120).

Income Statement Terms

Additional terms are defined in the *Business Terms Glossary* included on pages 170–171.

- **Gross turnover**: Total sales from all product line categories before *any* costs.

- **Allowances**: Amounts deducted from invoices for reasons such as buyer's speedy payment, large quantity purchases, or acceptance of faulty merchandise.

- **Net Sales**: Amount of total sales after deducting sales commissions, returns, and allowances.

- **Cost of Goods (COG):** Costs of raw materials, inventory, or other expenses directly associated with producing the product/service for sale.

- **Gross Profit:** Amount of sales after deducting commissions, returns, allowances, and cost of goods.

- **Depreciation**: Not a cash expenditure, but the amount allowed for tax purposes for the cost of ongoing wear-and-tear of fixed assets (facilities and equipment).

- **Pre-tax Profit**: Amount of income after deducting all costs of doing business.

- **Net Profit**: Amount of income after deducting all costs *plus* taxes.

QUICK**TIP**

Measuring Profitability

While an Income Statement is a reflection of a company's profit, it doesn't present the complete financial picture. For example, a business that's losing money on an annual basis could still be worth quite a lot because it owns valuable property—that will show up on the Balance Sheet. On the other hand, a profitable company may not have the cash flow to pay the bills. An Income Statement doesn't reveal either of these conditions.

INCOME STATEMENT

Year: 2006 (Actual through 8/31/06, projected 9–12/06)

	Jan	Feb	Mar	Apr	May
Income					
Gross Sales	£0	£2,000	£2,000	£5,000	£12,000
(Sales commissions)	0	0	0	0	350
(Returns and allowances)	0	0	0	0	0
Net Sales	0	2,000	2,000	5,000	11,650
(Cost of Goods)	0	324	324	812	1,946
GROSS PROFIT	0	1,676	1,676	4,188	9,704
OPERATING EXPENSES					
General and Administrative Expenses					
Salaries and wages	2,500	3,700	5,700	6,200	7,700
Employee benefits	275	275	510	510	510
Payroll taxes	210	310	505	505	505
Professional services	2,500	250	2,000	200	200
Rent	0	0	0	0	0
Maintenance	0	0	0	0	0
Equipment rental	250	250	250	250	250
Furniture and equipment purchase	0	0	0	410	0
Depreciation and amortisation	2,000	0	0	0	0
Insurance	400	0	0	200	0
Interest expenses	0	125	125	125	125
Utilities	250	60	125	210	160
Telephone service	100	50	100	100	120
Office supplies	450	125	215	185	125
Postage and shipping	210	80	310	65	450
Marketing and advertising	3,200	1,800	4,000	1,500	1,500
Travel	55	150	100	150	0
Entertainment	0	0	110	320	195
Technology	3,000	0	0	0	0
TOTAL OPERATING EXPENSES	15,400	7,175	14,050	10,930	11,840
Net Income before taxes	(15,400)	(5,499)	(12,374)	(6,742)	(2,136)
Taxes on income	0	0	0	0	0
NET PROFIT AFTER TAXES	(15,400)	(5,499)	(12,374)	(6,742)	(2,136)

June	July	Aug	Sep	Oct	Nov	Dec	TOTAL
£16,000	**£20,500**	**£28,000**	**£34,200**	**£41,800**	**£50,000**	**£21,500**	**£233,000**
750	775	1,235	1,500	1,850	2,200	950	£9,610
0	0	0	0	0	0	0	£0
15,250	**19,725**	**26,765**	**32,700**	**39,950**	**47,800**	**20,550**	**£223,390**
2,595	3,449	4,741	5,691	6,926	8,400	3,662	£38,870
12,655	**16,276**	**22,024**	**27,009**	**33,024**	**39,400**	**16,888**	**£184,520**
8,400	6,300	9,900	9,100	10,100	11,100	8,300	**£89,000**
510	510	700	700	700	700	700	**£6,600**
505	505	610	610	610	610	610	**£6,095**
200	200	1,200	200	200	200	200	**£7,550**
0	0	2,100	2,100	2,100	2,100	2,100	**£10,500**
0	0	120	120	120	120	120	**£600**
250	250	2,000	2,000	2,000	2,000	2,000	**£11,750**
0	0	0	0	0	0	0	**£410**
0	0	0	0	0	0	0	**£2,000**
0	200	1,000	350	550	350	350	**£3,400**
125	125	125	125	125	125	125	**£1,375**
200	175	260	220	210	180	150	**£2,200**
130	100	250	200	200	200	200	**£1,750**
85	110	1,100	250	250	250	250	**£3,395**
85	260	60	410	75	300	200	**£2,505**
300	1,500	1,750	2,000	250	2,000	250	**£20,050**
25	100	0	150	150	150	150	**£1,180**
200	75	85	50	50	50	50	**£1,185**
3,000	0	0	0	0	0	0	**£6,000**
14,015	**10,410**	**21,260**	**18,585**	**17,690**	**20,435**	**15,755**	**£177,545**
(1,360)	5,866	764	8,424	15,334	18,965	1,133	**£6,975**
0	0	0	0	0	0	1,046	**£1,046**
(1,360)	**5,866**	**764**	**8,424**	**15,334**	**18,965**	**87**	**£5,929**

INCOME STATEMENT—THREE-YEAR PROJECTION

	2006	2007	2008
Income			
Gross Sales	£233,000	£493,875	£818,615
(Commissions)	9,610	61,360	82,920
(Returns and allowances)	0	0	0
Net Sales	223,390	432,515	735,695
(Cost of goods)	38,870	62,133	86,610
GROSS PROFIT	184,520	370,382	649,085
OPERATING EXPENSES			
General and Administrative Expenses			
Salaries and wages	89,000	176,800	226,600
Employee benefits	6,600	15,000	21,600
Payroll taxes	6,095	15,000	20,000
Professional services	7,550	5,000	6,000
Rent	10,500	39,000	39,000
Maintenance	600	3,000	4,500
Equipment rental	11,750	38,000	48,000
Furniture and equipment purchase	410	500	0
Depreciation and amortisation	2,000	4,000	4,000
Insurance	3,400	4,200	5,500
Interest expenses	1,375	1,500	0
Utilities	2,200	5,000	5,500
Telephone service	1,750	1,200	2,000
Office supplies	3,395	5,000	6,000
Postage and shipping	2,505	3,600	5,000
Marketing and advertising	20,050	30,000	45,000
Travel	1,180	2,595	4,570
Entertainment	1,185	1,805	3,430
Technology	6,000	10,000	14,000
TOTAL OPERATING EXPENSES	177,545	361,200	460,700
Net Income before taxes	6,975	9,182	188,385
Provision for taxes on income	1,046	1,377	56,720
NET INCOME AFTER TAXES	5,929	7,805	131,665

INCOME STATEMENT					
	January	February	March	April	May
For Year _____					
INCOME					
Gross Sales					
(Commissions)					
(Returns and allowances)					
Net Sales					
(Cost of Goods)					
GROSS PROFIT					
OPERATING EXPENSES					
General and Administrative Expenses					
Salaries and wages					
Employee benefits					
Payroll taxes					
Professional services					
Marketing and advertising					
Rent					
Equipment rental					
Maintenance					
Depreciation					
Insurance					
Telephone service					
Utilities					
Office supplies					
Postage and shipping					
Travel					
Entertainment					
Interest on loans					
Other (insert additional expense here)					
Other (insert additional expense here)					
TOTAL OPERATING EXPENSES					
Net income before taxes					
Provision for taxes on income					
NET PROFIT AFTER TAXES					

June	July	August	September	October	November	December	TOTAL

2. Develop your Cash-Flow Projection

On a day-to-day basis, your Cash-Flow Projection is your most important financial analysis. It shows how much money you have coming into your business and how much going out. This 'flow' indicates whether you'll have enough cash to pay your bills.

The Cash-Flow Projection is not about profit—that shows up on the Income Statement. And it's not about the overall value of your company—that appears on the Balance Sheet. It's about how much money you have in the bank. It's a real-life picture of your cash situation.

Cash-Flow Projections are particularly important for seasonal businesses, those with large inventories, and businesses that sell primarily on credit. You must plan for the lag time between buying materials, making sales, and actually receiving cash.

In preparing Cash-Flow Projections, existing businesses should review past financial records to determine actual income and expense patterns. New businesses can check with others in their industry to gauge typical payment patterns.

The Cash Crunch

Even profitable businesses can easily get into a cash crunch, so keep an eye on your bank balance. Many businesses—especially growing companies—spend more than they receive on a month-by-month basis. After all, you typically have to pay for raw materials months before you're going to receive payment for the finished product. This delay presents a tricky problem for entrepreneurs, and most businesses use lines of credit or other financing tools to manage their cash-flow needs.

Cash-Flow Terms

- **Cash Sales:** Sales made where the income is received immediately. These can include credit card sales because the revenue is deposited in the company's bank within days.

- **Collections:** Income collected from accounts receivable—sales made on credit in a previous period.

- **Interest Income:** Cash received from interest-bearing accounts.

- **Loan Proceeds:** Cash received as a result of taking out a loan, credit card advance, or other credit line.

- **Equity Capital Investments:** Cash received from investors in return for a share of ownership (equity).

- **Owner's Draw:** Money paid to owner instead of (or in addition to) a salary. Common for sole traders.

- **Opening Cash Balance:** The amount of money in the bank or account at the beginning of the period (month/year/quarter)—the same as the previous period's Ending Cash Balance.

CASH-FLOW PROJECTION

Year: 2006

	Jan	Feb	Mar	Apr	May
CASH RECEIPTS					
Income from Sales					
Cash sales	£0	£2,000	£2,000	£5,000	£12,000
Collections	0	0	0	0	0
Total Cash from Sales	0	2,000	2,000	5,000	12,000
Income from Financing					
Interest income	0	0	0	0	0
Loan proceeds	15,000	0	0	6,000	10,000
Equity Capital Investments	20,000	0	10,000	0	0
Total Cash from Financing	35,000	0	0	6,000	10,000
Total Cash Receipts	35,000	2,000	12,000	11,000	22,000
CASH DISBURSEMENTS					
Expenses					
Cost of goods	0	324	324	812	1,946
Operating expenses	15,400	7,175	14,050	10,930	11,840
Commissions/returns & allowances	0	0	0	0	350
Loan payments	0	125	125	125	125
Income tax payments	0	0	0	0	0
Other expenses/equip purchase	10,000	0	0	0	0
Reserve	0	0	0	0	0
Owner's draw	0	0	0	0	0
Total Cash Disbursements	25,400	7,624	14,499	11,867	14,261
Net Cash Flow	9,600	(5,624)	(2,499)	(867)	7,739
Opening Cash balance	0	9,600	3,976	1,477	610
Cash receipts	35,000	2,000	12,000	11,000	22,000
Cash disbursements	(25,400)	(7,624)	(14,499)	(11,867)	(14,261)
Ending Cash Balance	9,600	3,976	1,477	610	8,349

June	July	Aug	Sep	Oct	Nov	Dec	TOTAL
£12,000	15,500	19,800	20,000	30,800	35,000	15,500	**£169,600**
4,000	5,000	8,200	14,200	11,000	15,000	6,000	**£63,400**
16,000	**20,500**	**28,000**	**34,200**	**41,800**	**50,000**	**21,500**	**£233,000**
0	0	0	0	0	0	0	**£0**
0	0	4,000	0	0	0	0	**£35,000**
0	0	0	0	0	0	0	**£30,000**
0	**0**	**4,000**	**0**	**0**	**0**	**0**	**£65,000**
16,000	**20,500**	**32,000**	**34,200**	**41,800**	**50,000**	**21,500**	**£298,000**
2,595	3,449	4,741	5,691	6,926	8,400	3,662	**£38,870**
14,015	10,410	21,260	18,585	17,690	20,435	15,755	**£177,545**
750	775	1,235	1,500	1,850	2,200	950	**£9,610**
125	125	125	125	125	5,125	10,125	**£16,375**
0	0	0	0	0	0	0	**£0**
0	0	0	0	0	0	0	**£10,000**
0	0	0	0	0	5,000	5,000	**£10,000**
0	0	0	0	0	0	0	**£0**
17,485	**14,759**	**27,361**	**25,901**	**26,591**	**41,160**	**35,492**	**£262,400**
(1,485)	**5,741**	**4,639**	**8,299**	**15,209**	**8,840**	**(13,992)**	**£35,600**
8,349	**6,864**	**12,605**	**17,244**	**25,543**	**40,752**	**49,592**	**£0**
16,000	20,500	32,000	34,200	41,800	50,000	21,500	**£298,000**
(17,485)	(14,759)	(27,361)	(25,901)	(26,591)	(41,160)	(35,492)	**(£262,400)**
6,864	**12,605**	**17,244**	**25,543**	**40,752**	**49,592**	**35,600**	

CASH-FLOW PROJECTION	January	February	March	April	May
For Year _____					
CASH RECEIPTS					
Income from Sales					
Cash Sales					
Collections					
Total Cash from Sales					
Income from Financing					
Interest Income					
Loan Proceeds					
Equity Capital Investments					
Total Cash from Financing					
Other Cash Receipts					
TOTAL CASH RECEIPTS					
CASH DISBURSEMENTS					
Inventory					
Operating Expenses					
Commissions/Returns & Allowances					
Capital Purchases					
Loan Payments					
Income Tax Payments					
Investor Dividend Payments					
Owner's Draw					
TOTAL CASH DISBURSEMENTS					
NET CASH FLOW					
Opening Cash Balance					
Cash Receipts					
Cash Disbursements					
ENDING CASH BALANCE					

CASH-FLOW PROJECTION							
June	July	August	September	October	November	December	TOTAL

3. Generate your Balance Sheet

If you're new to business, the Balance Sheet is likely the most perplexing of the major financial statements. It measures the overall value of your company at a particular time, but this can seem far less tangible than your profits (seen in your Income Statement) or actual cash (appearing in your Cash-Flow Projection).

The Balance Sheet itself is divided into two parts:

- The top part, where you list all your assets, such as cash, inventory, real estate, equipment, vehicles, and accounts receivable.

- The bottom part, where you total your liabilities, including accounts payable, loans, and payroll. The remaining amount (if any) is figured to be the *net worth*, expressed as shareholders' equity or retained earnings.

The final amounts for each part should be exactly equal—or *balance*.

The Balance Sheet presents investors and lenders with a snapshot of how much your company is worth, especially if it had to be sold. It shows the value of all tangible property and the extent of all debt. The value of some companies' assets may far exceed their profits, while other companies may show a profit but have heavy long-term debt.

Balance-Sheet Terms

- **Current Assets:** Anything your company has that can be turned into cash relatively quickly, including accounts receivable, inventory, and cash itself.

- **Fixed Assets:** Any tangible property your company owns that could be turned into cash more slowly, including real estate, equipment, and vehicles.

- **Current Liabilities:** Any accounts payable or other bills, debts, or financial obligations that must be paid relatively soon.

- **Long Term Liabilities:** Any financial obligations that must be paid over time, such as mortgages, loans, and equipment loans.

- **Net Worth:** The value of the company after deducting all liabilities from all assets.

- **Paid-In Capital:** Capital received from investors, as opposed to capital generated by the operations of a company.

BALANCE SHEET

For ComputerEase, Inc.
For Year Ending: December 31, 2007

ASSETS
Current Assets

Cash	£35,600	
Accounts Receivable	17,200	
Inventory	2,100	
Prepaid expenses	780	
Total Current Assets		**£55,680**

Fixed Assets

Land	0	
Buildings	0	
Furniture / equipment	10,000	
Less Accumulated Depreciation	(2,000)	
Total Fixed Assets		**£8,000**
Other Assets		0
TOTAL ASSETS		**£63,680**

LIABILITIES
Current Liabilities

Accounts Payable	8,675	
Accrued Payroll	3,050	
Taxes Payable	295	
Short-Term Notes Payable	5,000	
Total Current Liabilities		**£17,020**

Long-Term Liabilities

Long-Term Notes Payable	15,000	
Total Long-Term Liabilities		**£15,000**

Net Worth

Paid-In Capital	31,660	
Retained earnings	0	
Total Net Worth		**£31,660**
TOTAL LIABILITIES AND NET WORTH		**£63,680**

BALANCE SHEET

Your Company Name

Quarter _____ Year _____

ASSETS

Current Assets

Cash _____

Accounts Receivable _____

Inventory _____

Other Current Assets _____

Total Current Assets _____

Fixed Assets

Land _____

Facilities _____

Equipment _____

Computers & Telecommunications _____

(Less Accumulated Depreciation) _____

Total Fixed Assets _____

Other Assets _____

TOTAL ASSETS _____

LIABILITIES

Current Liabilities

Accounts Payable _____

Accrued Payroll _____

Taxes Payable _____

Short-Term Notes Payable _____

Total Current Liabilities _____

Long-Term Liabilities

Long-Term Notes Payable _____

Other Long-Term Liabilities _____

Total Long-Term Liabilities _____

NET WORTH

Paid-In Capital _____

Retained Earnings _____

Total Net Worth _____

TOTAL LIABILITIES AND NET WORTH _____

4. Show your Sources and Use of Funds

If you are seeking outside financing—loans or investments—you'll need to prepare one more key financial document: the Sources and Use of Funds statement. Your financing sources naturally want to know how much money you need, where you plan to get it, and what you're going to do with the money you raise. They also want to see if you've contributed any of your own money.

The Sources and Use of Funds statement can be a relatively simple one-page (or less) listing. Your task here is to assure investors and lenders that:

- You have specific plans for the money you raise

- They are aware of all the sources of funds you're seeking or have received

- You are not thoughtlessly taking on debt or giving up equity

- Ideally, you are using the money to help your business grow

Sources and Use of Funds Terms

- **Equity Financing:** Money raised from investors who receive a share of the company's ownership in return for their funds. These divide into business angels who will offer smaller amounts and have some input into the company and venture capitalists who will invest millions and be interested chiefly in a financial return.

- **Debt Financing:** Money raised by taking on loans, leases, mortgages, or other financial obligations. Funders receive additional interest payments as well as return of their initial capital in exchange for their funds.

- **Capital Expenditures**: Purchase of tangible property, such as real estate, equipment, and vehicles.

- **Working Capital**: Funds used for ongoing operating expenses of the business, including payroll, administrative and operating expenses, and marketing.

SOURCES AND USE OF FUNDS

Note: The total amount of financing being sought is £80,000 in equity financing. The company prefers that this entire amount be secured from only one investor. It is expected that these funds will be received and expended in early 2007. Thus the £80,000 is *not* reflected in the 2006 financial statements, but rather in the three-year projected income statement (page 120).

SOURCES OF FUNDS

Equity Investment	£80,000

USE OF FUNDS

Capital Expenditures

Leasehold Improvements	£ 5,000
Purchase of Equipment and Furniture	15,000
Total Capital Expenditures	**20,000**

Working Capital

Purchase of Inventory	5,000
Staff Expansion	25,000
Additional Marketing Activities	15,000
Other Business Expansion Activities	15,000
Total Working Capital	**60,000**

TOTAL USE OF FUNDS	**£80,000**

Answer the questions below to develop your 'Sources and Use of Funds' statement.

SOURCES OF FUNDS

What is the total amount of financing you are seeking (investments and loans)?

How much are the principals investing?

How much will be in the form of equity investment from others?

How much will be in the form of debt financing, specifically bank loans?

What other forms of debt financing will you be seeking? (Include equipment, mortgage, and vehicle loans/leases.)

What other sources of funds are you seeking, if any?

USE OF FUNDS

How much are you going to spend on capital expenditures (such as real estate, equipment, or computers)? Specify use and cost.

How much are you going to spend on inventory?

How much are you going to spend on working capital to run your business (for example, marketing, staff, and operating expenses)?

5. Consider preparing additional supporting financial statements

Before you develop the four key financial statements, you may find it very helpful to create separate forecasts for a few major components of your income and expenses. If you're using your business plan for internal company planning, these planning tools are particularly useful.

If you're developing your business plan primarily to seek outside financing, you don't necessarily need to prepare these statements. However, doing so will help you find the numbers you need to put in your Income Statement and Cash-Flow Projection.

Sales Projections

How many sales are you going to make? When? For how much? Forecasting your sales is obviously critical for understanding how much money you're going to have. Break down your projected sales by product line, on a month-by-month basis. Indicate how much you're going to pay in sales commissions, figure an amount for returns and discounts, and then calculate the cost of goods. This gives you revenue numbers to put in your Income Statement.

Staffing Budget

In many companies, the single biggest expense is the cost of employees. But it's often very frustrating (especially to investors) to see just one big number on the 'Salaries' line of a financial statement. Instead, it's helpful to break down your personnel costs by category (management, production, administrative, and marketing, for example), indicating how many employees you'll have in each category and what they'll cost. This also gives you numbers to put in both your Income Statement and your Cash-Flow Projection.

Marketing Budget

If marketing is a major expense for your company, you may want to itemise how you plan on spending your marketing and advertising money. This budget can be helpful to you in your own internal planning even if you don't include it with the business plan you prepare for outside investors or lenders.

Your financial forms are a critical part of your business plan. Investors and lenders will turn to your financial statements quickly to measure your company's profitability and to see how you earn and spend your money. The four most important financial documents are your Income Statement, Cash-Flow Projection, Balance Sheet, and if you're seeking financing, your Sources and Use of Funds statement. If you're unfamiliar—or uncomfortable—with preparing financial forms, get assistance from an accountant or bookkeeper.

Putting Your Business Plan on Show

Once your written business plan is reviewed positively, you may be asked to meet with readers of your plan (such as potential funders) and give a presentation. It's likely that you'll want to prepare a PowerPoint or other presentation for that meeting.

This presentation should highlight the most compelling aspects of your business and answer questions such as:

☐ What is your business concept?

☐ What is the size and nature of your market?

☐ What's happening with your competition?

☐ Who's on your team?

☐ What are your financial projections?

☐ What kind of growth do you project?

For more guidance, see *Winning Presentation In A Day*.

Presentation
Pointers

Looks matter. While your plan will ultimately be judged on the quality of your business concept and your strategies for achieving goals, you also want to make sure it gives the best first impression possible. The way you prepare and present the document is itself an indicator of your professionalism. A polished plan sheds a favourable light on your company; a sloppy or incomplete presentation works against you.

Length of Your Plan

Don't burden your business plan readers with excess verbiage. Keep your business plan as short as is reasonable. Most businesses can keep their plans under twenty pages; those with particularly complex concepts or products should try to limit the plan to thirty-five pages maximum. Uncomplicated small businesses may not need twenty pages, but anything less than ten may seem a bit light. You can place additional information in appendices.

Format and Layout

- **Choose a clear font.** Most software programs offer many choices of fonts or typefaces. Choose one that's easy to read and professional in appearance. Generally, serif fonts (the kind with small lines or 'feet' at the edges of each letter) make large amounts of text more readable, so choose this style for the body of your plan. Consider Garamond, Palatino, and Times New Roman.

Sans serif fonts (those without 'feet') work well for headings and subheads, especially in a bold or condensed style. Try Arial, Franklin Gothic, or Verdana.

- **Use no more than two fonts in your plan**, and be restrained in your use of italics, boldface, and underlining. In terms of font size, 10- to 12-point type is best for body text; 12- to 14-point works well for headings and subheads.

Serif Fonts:	Sans Serif Fonts:
Garamond	Arial
Palatino	Franklin Gothic
Times New Roman	Verdana

Graphs and Charts

Graphs and charts are excellent tools for communicating important or impressive information. Place charts of half-page size or less within the text to capture your readers' attention. Produce some or all of your charts or graphs in colour for more impact.

Since graphs and charts—especially those in colour—attract attention, make certain you include only the most important or compelling information in the form of graphs or charts.

Here are some different types of charts you can use to help convey specific information.

Bar charts are useful when demonstrating trends or drawing comparisons:

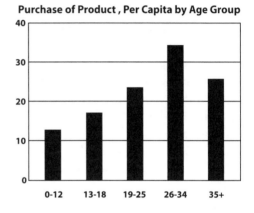

Purchase of Product , Per Capita by Age Group

Pie charts are ideal for showing the specific breakdowns of products sold, markets, etc.:

Store Sales by Product Category

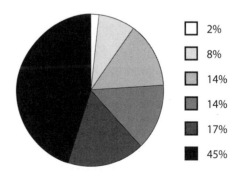

- ☐ 2%
- ☐ 8%
- ☐ 14%
- ☐ 14%
- ☐ 17%
- ■ 45%

Flow charts illustrate development patterns and organisation of authority:

Company Work Flow

Binding

You can have your business plan bound for a few pounds at most copy centres. This will give your plan a more polished, professional appearance. If you decide to use presentation folders or report covers instead (available at stationers), choose a business-like colour, such as black, grey, or dark blue. Label the front of your plan or use a clear cover with a title page. Readers should be able to see the name of your business without opening the plan.

Cover Sheet

Your cover sheet is the first thing readers will see when they open your plan. Make a good first impression with a clean, businesslike design. Your cover sheet should include:

- **Company name.**

- **Company logo**, if you have one.

- The words '**Business Plan**' in a prominent spot.

- The **name, address, phone number, and e-mail address** of the contact person

- **The date.** To be sure your plan doesn't look outdated, consider including only the year—or create a new cover sheet each time you send out the plan.

- **Copy number.** Number each copy of the plan you send out, and keep track of which reader (or institution) received it.

- **A disclaimer.** If you are circulating your plan to outside funding sources, you need to indicate that the business plan itself is not an offering of stock in the company. A disclaimer can protect you from legal problems and help protect the confidentiality of your plan.

A disclaimer might look like this:

This document is for information only and is not an offering for sale of securities of the Company. Information disclosed herein should be considered proprietary and confidential. The document is the property of _____ Company and may not be disclosed, distributed, or reproduced without the express written permission of _____ Company.

Consult a solicitor for proper wording.

Appendix

An appendix allows you to include information at the end of your plan without bogging down the essential sections with too much detail. Some types of information you can include:

- **Positive coverage.** If your company has received any positive coverage in news articles or industry journals, supply copies or clippings.

- **Letters of Intent.** Any indication from customers or potential customers of their intent to do business with you— or such letters from potential strategic partners.

- **List of locations.** Useful if you have many different stores or branches.

- **Manufacturing descriptions.** Floor plans, flow charts, or other visual representations that describe your manufacturing process.

- **Marketing collateral.** Brochures, leaflets, and photos of packaging. You can also include market research reports and other industry data here.

- **Photos, Illustrations, Graphs, and Charts.** Any images showing new technology, unique packaging, impressive industry information (charts or graphs), or other highlights of your business that are better presented visually.

- **Technical information.** If you're developing a new technology, data sheets and other descriptions (which may be too lengthy or technical for the plan itself) may be helpful here.

Cover Letter

You must include a cover letter with any business plan you send or deliver to a potential funding source. The cover letter will probably be read before the recipient opens the business plan itself, so make certain it entices the reader to give careful consideration to your business.

If you are sending your business plan to someone who has requested it, your cover letter should indicate that fact: You can start with a simple sentence, such as

It was a pleasure meeting you last week. As you requested, I'm sending you a copy of my business plan, for my company,
_____.

Then continue to briefly describe your business.

If you don't know the recipient of your plan personally, but someone you know is connected to that recipient (an intermediary), the best way to start a cover letter is with this sentence:

_____ *(name of intermediary)*
suggested that I contact you regarding my
business, _____
(name of business), a _____
(type of business).

For example, the first sentence might read:

Phil Turner suggested that I contact you regarding my business, AAA Ltd, a food products and service company.

This immediately draws attention to the person connecting you to the funding source and gives you a measure of credibility.

Next, indicate why you (or the intermediary) feel that the recipient is an appropriate funding source. Continuing with the example above, the next sentence might read:

He knows of your experience in funding food product companies and believes you might find AAA, Inc. of interest.

If you don't have an intermediary and you haven't met the funder yourself, your first sentence should state the name and nature of your company and why you have chosen to send your plan to the recipient. It should read something like:

Knowing of your interest in funding food product companies, I am enclosing a copy of the business plan for AAA Ltd. We are an established food products and service company now seeking financing to enable us to expand operations.

Regardless of how—or how well—you know the recipient of your business plan, your cover letter should state:

- Why you've chosen the particular funder to receive your plan.

- The nature of your business.

- The developmental stage of your business.

- The amount of funds sought.

- Whether you are looking for an investment or a loan.

- The terms of the deal, if appropriate.

Keep your cover letter brief like the sample opposite. It should motivate the recipient to read your plan, not replace the plan itself.

Cover Letter Sample

Ms. Tamara Pinto
335 Crowborough Road
London SW17

Dear Ms. Pinto:

My solicitor, Mr. Kenneth Pollock, suggested I write to you regarding my business, ComputerEase. I am currently seeking an investor, and I believe that this company would coincide with your interest in technology-related service businesses.

ComputerEase is positioned to take advantage of the market opportunities presented in the corporate software training field. This is a relatively new field, and no companies yet dominate the market. ComputerEase, through a professional approach to marketing, experienced management, and an emphasis on outstanding customer support and service, can become the premier provider of software training in the Edinburgh area. From that base, the company will be able to expand to become a regional force.

We are seeking £80,000. We anticipate this will be the sole round of funding. The funds will be utilised to add one training centre location, expand staff, and increase marketing activities.

I appreciate your consideration of the business plan for ComputerEase. I will telephone in approximately 10 days to see if you have any questions or to discuss how we may proceed.

Thank you.

Sincerely,

Scott E. Connors
President

Final Touches

The best business plans show up on their readers' desks with a clean design; clear, concise content; and an easy-to-navigate structure. Consider these additional guidelines for polishing and packaging your document.

- **Have it edited.** Ask someone with a good command of the English language to edit and proofread your business plan. After developing the plan yourself, you may find it difficult to catch typos and other grammatical problems on your own. You'll also want to see how others interpret your prose.

- **Include a table of contents.** If your plan is longer than ten pages, include a table of contents to help your readers quickly locate sections that interest them. Place it immediately after your cover sheet and before your Executive Summary.

Sending It Out

Before you drop your plan in the mail to any new financing source, give it another read-through, and if necessary, update it. Revise the plan to reflect recent developments (including new personnel), and bring financial information up to the close of the last month or quarter. Avoid printing too many copies at once so you're not tempted to send out an old plan just to get through the stack.

With investors and lenders in particular, your business plan is your calling card. Make sure its presentation puts the best face on your business and helps move your company closer to its goals.

Following Up

Your job is not done once you have sent out your business plan; you'll have to follow up with the recipients to make sure you actually receive an answer from your potential funding sources. Some banks or investors tell you exactly when you can expect to hear from them. Others are far less diligent in their communication. Don't be surprised if you're the one who has to take the initiative.

Don't become a pest, however. Keep your inquiries brief and professional, and don't contact potential funders too frequently. You can call for the first time about a week after sending your plan to make sure the plan has been received. During this first call, it's certainly appropriate to ask when you can expect to hear from the funding source or when you may call back. It's also acceptable to request an appropriate time to follow up again: 'May I call back in two weeks to check on my plan's progress?'

Email and Voicemail

Much of your interaction with potential funding sources will be through email and voicemail messages. Prepare what you want to say before you pick up the phone or hit the 'Send' button.

Keep all your initial or uninvited emails and voice mails short. You have a better chance of having your message read or listened to if it is not too long. If you've worked on your 'elevator pitch' (see page 151), you should be able to quickly explain the nature of your business.

If you have the name of an intermediary who suggested you contact the funding source, use that name right away, whether in a voice mail or email. In an email message, you might put the intermediary's name in the 'Subject' line to make it more likely the recipient will open your message.

For a voice mail message, state the nature of your call and your business up front and then clearly and slowly tell the listener how they can reach you. Always indicate that you will also phone back. That gives you an opening to call again without seeming too pushy.

If you're trying to make initial contact with a potential funder, your voice mail message might be something like:

Phil Turner suggested I call you about my new food products and service company, AAA Ltd. Phil thought our approach to growth and our already-established customer base would interest you. I'd appreciate the chance to speak with you. I can be reached at 0602-555-1000 or you can email me at arnie at aaa.co.uk. I will also try you again in a couple of days. Thank you.

Your email message can be very similar to your voicemail. It should be short and direct, and you should provide a way for someone to contact you by phone. You can include the address of your Web site, if you have one up and running and you're willing to have the potential funder see it before they've talked to you. Refrain from using any attachments, especially in your first contact. Be careful not to be too vague in your 'Subject' line. Don't use subjects such as 'Great Business Opportunity' or 'New Business Venture.' You don't want your recipient to think your message is spam and delete it without ever opening it.

The 'Elevator Pitch'

Before you meet with bankers, investors, or others, you need to work on developing your 'elevator pitch.' An elevator pitch is the term used for a very brief description of a company that an entrepreneur could give in the time it would take to ride up an elevator (and not an elevator in a skyscraper!). In your elevator pitch, you describe your company's product or service, market, and competitive advantages. An 'elevator pitch' shows you understand your business. (If you're unclear about your strategic position, you'll still be mumbling as you pass the fifteenth floor.)

You'll use your elevator pitch over and over: in emails to prospective financing sources, to introduce yourself and your company at networking events, to describe your business to potential customers. So take a few moments to begin to develop your own elevator pitch.

My Company:

Named:

Does:

Serves Which Market:

Makes Money By:

Is Like What Other Companies:

Will Succeed Because It:

Aims to Achieve:

Nine Sure-Fire Ways
to Ruin Your Business Plan

1. Make basic mistakes

Leave out key information or get basic facts wrong, and you'll mess up your entire business plan. Do your homework so you're familiar with standard industry practices. Educate yourself about distribution channels, price mark-ups, regulations, and legal and accounting matters. One error can ruin all your projections and assumptions.

2. Underestimate the competition

The worst thing you can say in a business plan is 'There is no competition'. No matter how unique or terrific your product or service, if you don't have competition, it means there's no market for what you're selling. Be sure to consider potential future competition once you've proven the concept.

3. Overestimate sales

When you launch a product or service that's better, faster, or cheaper than the competition's, it's natural to assume customers will beat a path to your door. They won't. Be realistic, even conservative, about how difficult it will be to build a customer base and how long it will take.

4. Plan more than one business at a time

Even though your business may eventually have a number of revenue streams, concentrate on one part of it at a time. Show you can be successful in one area before branching out.

5. Go it alone

Nobody can build a successful business alone. Strategic alliances, particularly with strong existing businesses, can improve your chances of success. And if you want your business to grow, you'll need to attract and keep capable management and personnel. Show you can work well and creatively with others to leverage your resources.

6. Use 'phantom' numbers

Don't use financial projections just because they sound good. Don't use 'boilerplate' numbers: industry averages might not apply in your situation. Be able to substantiate where you got your numbers and why you made your financial assumptions. Always overestimate expenses and underestimate income.

7. Forget a 'Sources and Use of Funds' statement

Financing sources want to see exactly how much money you'll need, how you intend to use it, what money you're contributing, and whether you are expecting to get funds from other sources. If you don't include this information in a clear, concise format, you'll confuse potential investors or lenders.

8. Omit an exit

While you may plan on running your business forever, others who invest in your company want to know how they'll get their money out. It's usually not enough for them to just get an annual return; they will want a way to make their original investment 'liquid'.

9. Lie

This is the best way to get a business plan rejected, increase the chances of your business failing, and ruin your reputation. While every business plan is developed with a certain degree of optimism, when the plan becomes fiction, you're in trouble.

The Experts Speak

Wouldn't it be wonderful if you could enter the minds of the people who will read your business plan—if you could learn what kinds of plans they read, what kinds they reject, and exactly what compels them to give a plan a thumbs up or a thumbs down?

Now you can. On the following pages, you'll find interviews with four people who read business plans for a living: two private equity investors, a venture capitalist, and a business angel.

They'll tell you in their own words:

● What kinds of information different financing professionals look for in a plan.

● What sections they turn to first.

● What they want to know about your team, your business and your market.

● What aspects of a plan's presentation they like—and dislike.

● What could destroy your chances of getting financing or meeting your other objectives.

Some of the experts take you beyond the plan review, explaining what happens after a plan is accepted. They provide valuable information on the kind of involvement they seek in the companies they finance—as well as how the ongoing professional relationship between the entrepreneur and the financing individuals or institution really works.

Before you take your plan to your readers, learn from the experienced experts interviewed here. Their ideas will help you create a winning plan, determine exactly who should read it, and significantly boost its chances for success.

Mark Turner, Partner at ISIS Equity Partners LLP

Mark joined ISIS Equity Partners LLP (ISIS) in 2001 to work in the portfolio management function. He currently sits on the investee boards of LBM, The Art Group and Enotria. He has worked on several investments which have been taken through to exit. These include Americana, Thomas Sanderson and Blue 8. Mark also led the flotation of Staffline in 2004.

ISIS is a private equity house which invests in dynamic small- to medium-sized UK businesses run by entrepreneurial managers. Working in partnership with them, ISIS creates market leading companies that deliver excellent returns to all shareholders.

ISIS is passionate about backing businesses that display ambition and have strong growth prospects.

What sort of information do you look for in a business plan – and how do your needs differ from other sorts of lenders?

The type of information I would look for in a business plan include:

a) **Management.** I would be interested in obtaining more information about the business founder/s and management team. What is their career history? I would look for a strong business background and an understanding of their key achievements and failures. I don't want to see a chronological statement only.

b) **Market position of the company.** I would want to know more about the market and the market sectors being targeted. Who are the customers? Also, how does the company fit in with the market? Is the product or service being offered unique or distinct? Who are the competitors, their size and position in the market? Information about competitive products/services that are currently on the market or likely to emerge should also be included in this analysis.

c) **Market opportunity.** In this section I would be looking for a clear understanding of the market opportunities as they apply to the company. For instance, they may have plans to expand the product range or diversify into new markets.

d) Evidence of a **strategic framework for decision making.**

e) What is the **value strategy**? For instance, does the business plan link with shareholder value creation? How will shareholders get a return on their investment?

f)   **Financial plan.** As part of the financial analysis, I would expect to see: a summary of forecasts, profit forecast for five years, cash flow forecast for five years, forecast balance sheet for five years, historic numbers for four years, any assumptions behind the figures and details of the principal risks which would affect figures.

g)   **Operational structure and detail on key processes**. I'd want to know more about how the business operates. Where is it located? Who are the suppliers? Details about any facilities being utilised (e.g. manufacturing, R&D). What equipment is being used? Have specific IT, sales and marketing strategies been identified?

I suspect our requirements for the base business plan are similar to our competitors. However, once we have reached an agreement to invest in a business, we would work with management to build a detailed and in-depth business plan.

When you receive a plan, in what order do you read the various sections?

When I receive a business plan, I would read the various sections in the following order: management, market, strategy, financials and value creation.

What do you want to know about the competition?

Firstly, it is important to assess via the business plan that there is acceptance by management that they have competition!

Then I would look for evidence that management has an in-depth understanding of the competitive landscape. I would want to see an explanation of the differentiation between competitive players. A market map illustrating this point is always helpful and says a lot.

What do you want to know about the market?

The main point that I am interested in about the market at this early stage is 'how can company x create value in it?'

What do you consider 'red flags' or danger signs?

The red flags or danger signs that I'd look for in a business plan include declining gross margins, reliance on a supplier/s, high staff turnover, a complicated corporate history and an unclear or overcomplicated strategy.

What is the range of money you invest?

The money that ISIS invests ranges from £2m to £30m of equity.

What kinds of businesses most interest you?

ISIS invests in profitable small- to medium-sized UK businesses. ISIS looks for companies that are either already market leaders or have the ability to become market leaders, and which have management teams with strong entrepreneurial flair. ISIS focuses its investment activity in five sectors: business & financial services (http://www.isisep.com/sector/financial.cfm), consumer markets, healthcare & education (http://www.isisep.com/sector/healthcare.cfm), information technology (http://www.isisep.com/sector/it.cfm) and media. These are the sectors where ISIS has developed a deep understanding and strong networks.

What size of companies do you invest in?

ISIS invests in companies that are valued between £5m and £75m and companies that are seeking between £2m and £30m of equity.

Do you prefer that a company's finances come mainly from you or from many different sources?

A company's finances must mainly come from ISIS as we want to be the lead investor. ISIS also uses debt facilities from the banks.

What do you notice first about a plan's physical presentation?

The first thing I will notice about the physical presentation of a plan is if it is over-stylised.

What is a good length for a business plan?

A detailed 20 page presentation which has useful appendices is a good length for a business plan.

How much and what kind of supporting data should be included (such as studies, surveys, graphs and charts)

The inclusion of supporting data such as studies, surveys, graphs and charts are only useful if they have relevance to the value strategy.

How much time do you spend reading a plan?

The time I spend reading a plan depends on the plan. I can spend from one hour to many hours to a number of days where I may involve others when looking at a plan.

What type of involvement do you look for in the companies you finance?

The ISIS team are actively involved in the companies we finance. We will typically talk to the managing director and/or finance director once a week. We'll also take a seat on the board and bring expert advice and input to strategic issues.

Xavier Adam, Private Equity Investor

Xavier is MD of AMC and has worked on private equity and other deals for the last ten years – mainly in the US and Europe. These range from seed to significant market flotations.

What sort of information do you look for in a business plan – and how do your needs differ from other sorts of lenders?

- A good idea that will fly. What does the street think? Will people buy? Basic but vital questions.

- Experienced people.

- A track record of people, business and concept – what can my network tell me about the proposition?

- Appealing sector: is there a future here?

Other investment side personnel may be interested around 80–90% in the idea alone, with less emphasis on the other aspects. As these may be 'learned' at some stage. I like the whole package to be right.

When you receive a plan, in what order do you read the various sections?

Have a quick scan, then re-read at leisure. Usually look at the idea and what the people have done beforehand. Most plans come from people I know or have got to know through investment talks.

What do you want to know about the competition?

Their research and my research. Who it is, what they do, why this proposition is different (or not) and going to fly.

What do you consider 'red flags' or danger signs?

Over enthusiastic growth figures, especially in the early days, and when research is based on little, or, purely tertiary information.

What would make you reject a plan out of hand?

People that think they know more about the process than you, people who can't give straight and direct answers. People who allude in a 'clever' way to other offers, and look to play you off against these others.

What is the range of money you invest?

From seed to in excess of 100 million euros.

What kinds of businesses most interest you?

Media, Internet, technology. Some automotive. Western-based preferably – at least the aspects requiring investment. Businesses with longevity, not hyped up and flash in the pan. Medium- to long-term holds.

Do you prefer that a company's finances come mainly for you or from many different sources?

Either, but usually the latter, which is most often the case.

What do you notice first about a plan's physical presentation?

Is it straightforward? Are there spelling mistakes and typos? Does the concept come across in a simple and easy to understand manner?

What is a good length for a business plan?

Depends, but there is no point being excessively long for the sake of it.

How much and what kind of supporting data should be included (such as studies, surveys, graphs and charts)?

Anything primary is good, as are primary sources. If it is from a secondary source, then has it got credibility? e.g. The *FT*, a known expert or institution…

How much time do you spend reading a plan?

Initially around 20–30 minutes. If it seems a goer, around an hour at a later stage, making pencil marks on a hard copy, and listing *all* queries.

What type of involvement do you look for in the companies you finance?

Advisory. Ongoing relationship. Ability to use skills, knowledge and network to get the business where it wants/needs to be.

Maisy Ng, Venture Capitalist

Maisy Ng is a managing partner at Add Partners, a venture capital firm investing in ambitious, promising technology startups across Western Europe. She co-founded the company with more than ten years' technology and venture capital experience that spans Asian, American and European markets. Maisy was previously a senior manager at Vertex Management, the Singapore-based multinational private equity firm. There she was part of the pioneering team that established Vertex's European operations and headed their European office in London. Prior to that, Maisy worked for eight years in the semiconductor industry, where she was a chip designer in Silicon Valley and Singapore before moving into product marketing. Maisy is named as a co-inventor in six US technology patents.

What sort of information do you look for in a business plan – and how do your needs differ from other sorts of lenders?

Ideally, I'd like to come away after reading the plan with a strong sense that the company has the potential to be a really large business that can exit at a significant value in a few years' time.

A lot of business plans omit information about the exit scenarios. It is very important for a potential investor in the business to know that the management has an ambitious and realistic view towards exit and is motivated to exit within a reasonable time frame and at a good value.

When you receive a plan, in what order do you read the various sections?

I normally read the Executive Summary first to get an overall view of the business. Then I'll usually turn to the Executive Team biographies to get a sense of the backgrounds of the founders/executives.

Next I'll have a quick look at the financials. I'm more interested at this stage in knowing the current size/run-rate of the business rather than future projections. If all of these look interesting so far, I'll read in more detail the market and product sections.

What do you want to know about the competition?

Firstly, I'd like to know if there is competition. If there isn't, I'd like to know why – has the company cottoned onto something that no one else has? If so, that's fantastic! Or is the market so small or so far off in the future that no one else is interested to play in it?

Secondly, if competition exists, I'd like to know how the company stacks up against it. Can the company win in a head-to-head competition and emerge as the dominant player? In the event of an industry consolidation, will the company emerge to be a consolidator or just one of the victims?

Thirdly, I would be interested to know who are the adjacent competitors and the companies who offer substitutes rather than purely competitive products. Again, it will be important to figure out what role each might play as the industry evolves or when consolidation takes place.

What do you want to know about the market?

Does the market already exist? If so, at what stage is it – early adopter/early majority/late majority or already in harvest stage?

Or is the market newly emerging? Is it or will it be big enough for a large company to emerge?

What do you consider 'red flags' or danger signs?

- Small, niche target markets definitely will not do.

- Product or technology that does not appear to be defensible will raise serious questions.

- Unrealistic financial projections.

- Exit valuations or timeframes that sound too good to be true.

- Founder/management team profiles that seem to indicate that the key people have not stuck at anything for long.

Do you get many plans that are off the wall?

Not so much these days. We find that since the Internet bubble burst, most of plans we see are better thought through.

What would make you reject a plan out of hand?

Small niche target markets; 'outlandish' financial projections; questionable intellectual property – these are primary reasons why plans get rejected out of hand.

What is the range of money you invest?

We do anything from £250K to £5M ticket sizes but £1M to £1.5M in a single round is the sweet spot.

What kinds of businesses most interest you?

We like companies who are 'category definers' – i.e. companies who have the best shot at becoming the dominant player in a newly emerging market that will become very large. Such potentially large, new markets might emerge when there is a paradigm shift in technology or market forces within an industry.

What size of companies do you invest, and at what stage do you come in?

Add Partners has been most active in Series A & B (1st and 2nd institutional rounds), but in reality we can and will do all stages from pre-revenue Series A through to pre-IPO.

Do you prefer that a company's finances come mainly from you or from many different sources?

We are fairly agnostic about this. We do, however, like the cross-pollination of ideas that comes with having a few VCs on board. On the other hand, having too many investors can sometimes lead to a more complicated capital structure and/or a slower decision making process.

A good rule of thumb might be, for example, no more than two new investors per round.

Given that the relative fund size in Europe is smaller than that in the US, it would be prudent for companies to pick funds that have the ability to do follow-on investments in future rounds.

What do you notice first about a plan's physical presentation?

Layout and organisation of paragraphs and font size.

If the plan is sent by post, I would be concerned if it were printed on expensive paper or bound in an expensive cover!

What is a good length for a business plan?

No more than 20 pages.

How much and what kind of supporting data should be included (such as studies, surveys, graphs and charts)?

Only relevant data should be included. It's probably best not to clutter the business plan with too much supporting data. These can always be provided on request when the financier is going towards the due diligence phase.

How much time do you spend reading a plan?

A couple of hours.

What type of involvement do you look for in the companies you finance?

We typically take a board seat in each company we finance. Our style is that of an active, participatory and supportive non-executive role in the company. We are company builders. We will not shy away from asking difficult strategic questions and will work hard with the founder/management team to build value and exit at the right time.

Dominic Perks, Business Angel

Dominic Perks has been an investment banker at Morgan Stanley and Strategy Consultant at McKinsey and Co. He has investments currently in Careerability Ltd and holds a number of directorships.

What sort of information do you look for in a business plan – and how do your needs differ from other sorts of lenders?

I am interested in the people behind the plan – what are their real motivations? What are their experiences to date? How clear is their vision for this business? Have they failed yet? And what is at stake for them?

When you receive a plan, in what order do you read the various sections?

In the order provided – from beginning to end.

What do you want to know about the competition?

How strong are their management, and how are they capitalised. And – crucially – what would it take to beat them?

What do you want to know about the market?

Its growth potential. I am a strong believer in swimming with the tide.

What is the range of money you invest?

£20k to £2m

What kinds of businesses most interest you?

Businesses that can be truly distinctive in their market. In my experience there are three ways this can be achieved. Sometimes, the idea itself is enough; sometimes, the passion of an individual. Occasionally, the drive and determination of an individual or a team to make things work can create a special business. If you are lucky enough to have all three, you have a recipe for success.

What size of companies do you invest, and at what stage do you come in?

Three stages are of interest:

- Seed capital/start-up.

- Development capital/first/second round financing.

- Turnaround/recovery capital.

Do you prefer that a company's finances come mainly from you or from many different sources?

I prefer to do the financing myself – greater influence, cleaner governance and easier for the management team.

What is a good length for a business plan?

A one page summary is useful – if the message/idea and plan can't be condensed to one page then there's a problem. Thereafter, a detailed plan (20 pages +) with financial forecasts, can be reviewed.

How much and what kind of supporting data should be included (such as studies, surveys, graphs and charts)?

The more research that has been done the better. Every page/slide should have a key message which is supported by the data. Every page should be scrutinised with the question: 'So what?'.

How much time do you spend reading a plan?

Initially, 2 minutes. If I'm interested, 2 hours.

What type of involvement do you look for in the companies you finance?

I become a Board Director and look to provide strategic guidance and help companies in whatever way I can, using my skills and experiences and sharing my network.

Business Terms
Glossary

Angel: A private investor who invests personal funds in new enterprises.

Barriers to Entry: Conditions that make it difficult or impossible for new competitors to enter the market; examples include patents and extremely high start-up costs.

Board of Directors: The governing body of an incorporated company; this body has legal authority and responsibility for the business.

Capital: Funds/money to establish or run a business.

Cash Flow: The movement of money into and out of a company; actual income received and actual payments made out.

Collateral: Assets pledged in return for loans; examples include real estate and accounts receivable.

Corporation: A legal form of business that provides certain benefits for the company's owners, including protection from personal liability.

Cost of Goods: The direct costs to make or acquire products being sold; examples include the cost of raw materials or inventory.

Debt Financing: Raising funds for a business by borrowing, often in the form of bank loans.

Distributor: Company or individual that arranges for the sale of products from manufacturer to retail outlets; the proverbial 'middle man'.

Equity: Shares of stock in company; ownership interest in a company.

Gross Profit (also known as pre-tax profit): The amount of money earned after deducting the cost of goods but before deducting operating expenses.

Leasehold Improvements: Changes made to a rented store, office, or plant to make the location more appropriate for the conduct of the tenant's business.

Licensing Agreement: The granting of permission by one company to another to use its products, trademark, or name in a limited, particular manner.

Limited: Short for 'Limited Liability Company', a specific legal form for a company providing limited liability and pass-through tax treatment for the company's owners.

Liquid Asset: An asset that can be turned into cash quickly and easily; examples include publicly traded stock and cash on deposit in banks.

Market Share: The percentage of the total available customer base captured by a specific company.

Milestone: A company's particular business achievement, such as shipping a new product or reaching a specific level of sales.

Net Profit: The amount of money earned after costs of goods and all operating and marketing expenses (often figured before taxes and depreciation).

Non-executive Directors: A non-official group of advisors; with no legal authority or obligation.

Outsource: To have certain tasks done or products made by another company on a contract basis rather than having the work done by one's own company in-house.

Partnership: A relationship of two or more individuals to own or run a company without formal incorporation or the creation of a Limited Company.

Profit: The amount of money earned after expenses; it can be gross profit or net profit.

Profit Margin: The amount of money earned after expenses, usually expressed in percentage terms. Gross profit margin is the amount earned after deducting the cost of goods from total revenues; net profit margin is derived after deducting cost of goods plus operating expenses from total revenues.

Receipts: Funds coming into the company; the actual money paid to the company for its products or services; not necessarily the same as a company's total revenues.

Revenues: Total sales of a company before expenses. This is distinguished from profits or from receipts.

Sole Trader: A non-incorporated company owned and managed by one person.

Strategic Partnerships: An agreement with another company to undertake business endeavors together or on each other's behalf.

T/A: 'Trading as'. A company's trade name rather than the name under which it is legally incorporated; a company may be incorporated under the name XYZ Corporation but trade as 'The Dew Drop Inn'.

Venture Capitalist: Individual or firm who invests money in new enterprises; typically this money is invested in the venture capital firm by others, particularly institutional investors.

Working Capital: The cash available to the company for the ongoing operations of the business.

Business
Resources

Funding Sources

British Business Angel Association

www.bbaa.org.uk

Umbrella group representing business angels in the UK.

British Venture Capital Association

www.bvca.co.uk

The BVCA represents the vast majority of private venture capital firms in the United Kingdom.

Business Link

http://www.businesslink.gov.uk/bdotg/action/layer?topicId=1073858790

Government guidance on financing for your company.

European Venture Capital Association

www.evca.com

The EVCA represents over 950 venture capital firms in Europe.

Entrepreneurs' Sources

Enterprise Directorate

**http://www.dti.gov.uk/bbf/
small-business/**

Formerly the Small Business Service, this
is the Government's key resource for small
business owners.

Federation of Small Businesses

www.fsb.org.uk

Pressure group for small business owners, a
campaigning group for the interests of the
smaller trader.

Forum for Private Business

www.fpb.org.uk

The other leading pressure group for small
business owners.

Institute of Directors

www.iod.com

Members-only group for directors of incorporated or unincorporated businesses.

Microsoft Small Business Centre

www.bcentral.co.uk

Surprisingly large amount of independent
advice for businesses from a company
whose primary job is to sell software.

Index

Acknowledgments

Rhonda Abrams and The Planning Shop would like to thank:

Julie Vallone, who brought her constant professionalism, expert writing skills, easy-going personality and good humour to this project. Julie has been an outstanding addition to The Planning Shop team, and we look forward to a long working relationship with her.

Mireille Majoor, our Editorial Project Manager. Mireille has overseen the entire development process, managed too-tight schedules, and risen to the challenges of creating a new editorial process. We have benefited greatly from Mireille's knowledge of the publishing process, good humour, unending patience, and her occasional pun.

Arthur Wait, who is responsible for the look and feel of everything carrying The Planning Shop name. We are always amazed (though no longer surprised) at the range of his talent. As VP of Everything (not his real title, but it should be), Arthur has his hand in shaping the entire direction of The Planning Shop, as well as being its tech wizard.

Diana Van Winkle, who brought her graphic expertise to improving and refining the design of this book. Her rapid responses and professionalism made working with her a pleasure, and she shares in the credit for making this book as elegant and userfriendly as it is.

Deborah Kaye, the 'glue' that holds The Planning Shop together. Not only does Deborah manage all relations with the academic market, but she oversees operational issues and handles all the challenges that arise.

Brian Luce, who makes sure that the books get shipped, the phones get answered, the bills get sent, and otherwise handles the day-to-day administrative details of The Planning Shop's busy office.

The experts who provided such valuable, real-life insight into the business plan evaluation process: Tony Shipley, Patrick Sandercock, Phil Schlein, and Enzo Torresi. Special thanks to my good friend Phil, who has provided guidance and assistance for many years as well as being my standing date for Opening Day every year for the San Francisco Giants.

Kathryn Dean, who brought her eagle eye and expert judgment to the editing and proofing process, and who created the index in record time.

Finally, thanks for the company and support of the three amazing dogs at The Planning Shop: Cosmo, Ozzy, and Nana. Woof!

Julie Vallone would like to thank:

My daughter, Siena, for spilling juice on my keyboard when it was clearly time for a writer's break; our cats, Zoe, Squinky, Lola and Sappho, for keeping my feet and pages warm; and my husband Rick, for patiently putting up with the stacks of disheveled paper and books, scattered energy bar wrappers and thirty-four used coffee cups littering our dining table as deadline approached.

My gratitude also to designer and Web wizard Alan Luckow, who knows how to connect, and to the kind folks at Mr. Toots, The Ugly Mug, and Union coffee houses in Santa Cruz County, my satellite offices.

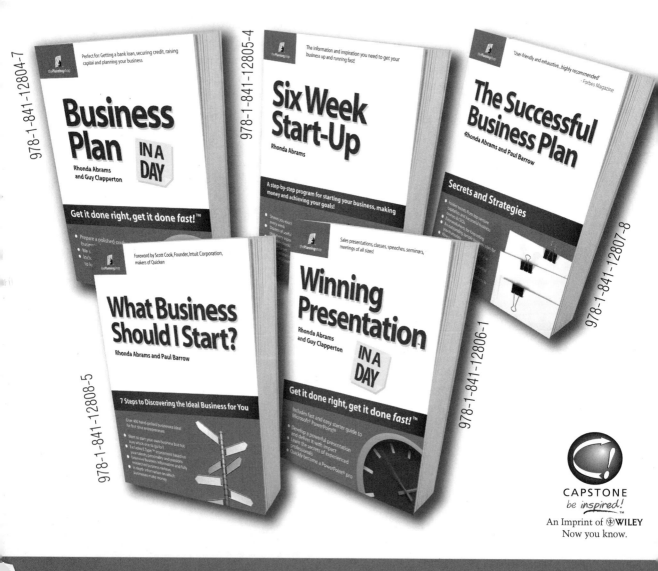